The

Reference

Shelf

China

Edited by Dimitri Cavalli

The Reference Shelf
Volume 74 • Number 5

The H.W. Wilson Company
2002

The Reference Shelf

The books in this series contain reprints of articles, excerpts from books, addresses on current issues, and studies of social trends in the United States and other countries. There are six separately bound numbers in each volume, all of which are usually published in the same calendar year. Numbers one through five are each devoted to a single subject, providing background information and discussion from various points of view and concluding with a subject index and comprehensive bibliography that lists books, pamphlets, and abstracts of additional articles on the subject. The final number of each volume is a collection of recent speeches, and it contains a cumulative speaker index. Books in the series may be purchased individually or on subscription.

Library of Congress has cataloged this title as follows:

China / edited by Dimitri Cavalli.
     p.cm.—(The reference shelf; v. 74, no. 5)
    Includes bibliographical references and index.
    ISBN 0-8242-1014-X (alk. paper)
    1. China—Politics and government—1976- I. Cavalli, Dimitri. II. Series.

DS779.26 .C47282002
951.06—dc21

2002028097

Visit H.W. Wilson's Web site: www.hwwilson.com

Printed in the United States of America

Contents

Preface

For nearly 1,000 years, people in the West have been fascinated with China, a vast and populous nation located "on the other side of the world." During the late Middle Ages and the Renaissance, Westerners followed the Silk Route in order to obtain the rare and beautiful fabrics woven by the Chinese, while in the 19th century, Europe and the United States eagerly sought lucrative concessions through trade with China, usually to China's detriment. The weak Manchu dynasty was unable to resist foreign incursions into its country. During 1839–43 and 1856–60, China fought and lost the Opium Wars with Great Britain, and trade with France, Germany, and the United States proved disadvantageous. War with Japan in 1894–95 further weakened China economically and militarily. The unrest which these humiliations created among the Chinese people culminated in the Boxer Uprising in 1900, a nationalist rebellion against all foreigners and alien influence in China.

During the 20th century, China underwent additional upheavals. The Manchu dynasty fell, bringing an end to imperial rule. A republican government ruled China until 1949, when the Communist forces of Mao Tse-tung seized power. Mao established a dictatorship that rivaled Nazi Germany and the Soviet Union under Josef Stalin in its brutality, repressiveness, and genocide. Some of the worst atrocities occurred during the Cultural Revolution, which began in 1966 as Mao's attempt to squelch opposition to the Communist Party and his authority. Millions of people from all walks of life—including many Communist leaders—were severely persecuted or killed for expressing ideas or acting in ways that Mao and his Red Guard deemed too "bourgeois."

For over 20 years, the United States sought to isolate China by refusing to recognize the Communist regime and keeping it out of the United Nations. The situation changed when President Richard Nixon made his historic visit to China in February of 1972. Nixon sought to exploit China's rivalry with the Soviet Union and expose China to Western influences, which he hoped would gradually turn it away from Communism. By the end of the decade, the United States had officially recognized the People's Republic of China and the two nations had established diplomatic relations.

After Mao's death in 1976, a new leader, Deng Xiaoping, introduced several reforms. Deng abandoned Mao's hard-line Marxist-Leninist ideology and encouraged the limited ownership of private property and a free market. Deng's reforms sparked economic growth and improved the standard of living for many people who had languished under Mao's policies. Deng's liberalization, however, did not extend to China's political system, which remained repressive and intolerant of any dissent. In 1989 Deng shocked the world by ordering the massacre of thousands of pro-democracy students in Beijing's Tiananmen Square.

Today, under President Jiang Zemin, China is one of the world's great powers, occupying a permanent seat on the United Nations' Security Council and boasting a strong military with a nuclear arsenal. A large population and substantial resources and capital also make China a formidable competitor in the global marketplace.

The articles collected in this book from a diverse group of sources provide a glimpse into present-day China. The first section discusses the prospects for the liberalization of China's political system and examines whether there is any chance that China could become a Western-style democracy. The second section looks at Chinese domestic issues, such as the economy, the morale of China's workers, crime, education, health care, and the plight of abandoned children. One article in this section also assesses the state of Hong Kong five years after the British transferred its administration to China. Section three focuses on human rights, detailing China's suppression of freedom of expression at the nation's major universities and the persecution of several religious groups. The fourth section analyses the present state of U.S.-Chinese relations. Despite the fears expressed by many that these nations are on the verge of a cold war, primarily due to their divergent views on China's treatment of Taiwan and the deployment by the United States of a missile defense shield, both countries have pledged publically to work towards maintaining friendly relations with one another. The fifth and final section offers a look at China's dealings with other states, including Russia, India, Pakistan, Japan, Taiwan, and the Vatican. An appendix follows with statistics and other important facts about the geography, economy, government, communications, transportation, and population of the People's Republic of China.

In conclusion, I would like to express my gratitude to the periodicals throughout the world that gave their generous permission to have their articles reprinted in this book, and to all those at the H.W. Wilson Company, whose assistance and work made this book possible, especially Lynn Messina, Sandra Watson, Jennifer Peloso, Norris Smith, Richard Joseph Stein, and Gray Young.

Dimitri Cavalli
October 2002

I. Is China Liberalizing?

Editor's Introduction

C hina is one of the last Communist regimes in the world—and certainly the largest. Unlike the much smaller Communist nations of Cuba and North Korea, however, China has distanced itself from Marxist-Leninist ideology in the last two decades and has introduced free market reforms that have sparked economic growth and improved the standard of living for many people. Despite these economic reforms, China remains a repressive state that outlaws independent political parties and persecutes many religious groups and political dissidents. Nevertheless, many analysts believe that successful economic reforms will eventually lead to political reform, possibly turning China from an authoritarian regime into a Western-style democracy that respects human rights and personal freedoms.

This section assess China's potential for evolving into a liberal democracy and identifies the forces at work for and against that liberalization. In her article for *Asiaweek.com*, Dorinda Elliott discusses how China's 2001 admission into the World Trade Organization (WTO) will cause the nation to institute liberal reforms. As a condition of admittance, China has agreed to implement the WTO's many protocols, rules, and regulations, which should bring sweeping changes to the country. The reforms should introduce competition into many inefficient, unproductive state-owned enterprises and allow many foreign companies to compete in China on a level playing field with domestic businesses. In the long run, China's membership in the WTO could create economic opportunities for millions of people, raise the standard of living, and improve the overall economy. As Elliott observes, "Beijing's challenge will be managing all the change—and preventing social unrest."

In their article "China's Coming Transformation," George Gilboy and Eric Heginbotham argue that China's economic reforms during the past 20 years have unleashed social forces that will dramatically change Chinese politics as a new generation of leaders takes power in the 21st century. Although they express doubt that China will become a democracy anytime soon, Gilboy and Heginbotham predict that China's new leaders will accelerate political reform to accommodate the social forces that are pushing the system toward change and to preserve the benefits of economic reform. The authors suggest that independent social organizations may be legitimized, giving citizen groups a greater voice in policymaking, and that "intraparty democracy" may develop— two reforms that "are as likely to throw China into domestic turmoil as they are to create a stable partial democracy."

During a tour of China, Peter Hadekel, the editorial-page editor of the Montreal *Gazette*, where he published the third article in this chapter, saw hope for the further establishment of liberal reforms. Hadekel believes that China's admission in the WTO and the growing investment in China's fledgling stock market by tens of millions of Chinese citizens will transform the country in the next ten years. Hadekel was especially impressed by the Shanghai High School, an elite boarding school that has produced many of China's political and military leaders. Although he was skeptical of the vice-principal's claim that students at the school are encouraged to think independently and draw their own conclusions, Hadekel reports that the students also spend hours surfing the Internet and can access Western media sites that provide alternatives to the government ideology. The students also have opportunities to master the English language and experience American culture through a joint summer exchange camp that the school runs with Harvard University in Cambridge, Massachusetts.

In Toronto's *National Post*, Michael A. Ledeen argues that free market reforms are changing China. However, he dissents from the view that economic reforms are laying the foundations for democracy. Instead, Ledeen suggests that China is making the transition from a Communist state to a fascist one. Ledeen asserts that despite free market reforms, China's leaders have not embraced capitalism. Although individual citizens are free to own private property and open businesses, the state still controls many large corporations. According to Ledeen, China is turning into a politically repressive "corporate state" that resembles Italy when it was ruled by the fascist dictator Benito Mussolini from 1922 to 1943.

The section closes with a profile by *Washington Times* reporter David R. Sands of Chinese Vice President Hu Jintao, who is expected to succeed President Jiang Zemin when he retires. Sands notes the uncertainty of many observers about Hu's stand on key issues affecting China. While some see him as a political reformer who has endorsed good relations with the United States, others view him as a party hard-liner, as exemplified in his support of the massacre of pro-democracy students in Tiananmen Square and his supervision of a brutal crackdown on political dissidents in Tibet, both in 1989.

Playing by the Rules[1]

By Dorinda Elliott
Asiaweek.com, December 7, 2001

Andy Lee is dumbfounded as he emerges from a board meeting in Beijing. Born in Chongqing, educated at Stanford University, Lee has returned to China to help the Academy of Sciences develop software standards for Chinese industry. Now, Lee, who once ran a software company in Silicon Valley, is spinning off a technology start-up with mainland colleagues, backed by venture capital from Intel and others. The meeting's agenda was simple enough: map out an organization chart. But for more than nine frustrating hours, Lee and his Academy of Sciences partners haggled over management structure and pay. Lee thought the chief executive officer should be the boss; the Chinese scientists lobbied for a four-member decision-making committee. Lee contended that pay should be based on merit; his colleagues wanted regimented salaries, with small, standardized jumps per rank. "It's quite socialist," says Lee of the organization chart finally agreed upon, which instead of the typical capitalist pyramid is square-shaped to reflect the four-man team at the top.

Perhaps it's appropriate that Lee's marathon meeting took place last month on the eve of China's entry into the World Trade Organization. As momentous an occasion as the world's biggest country agreeing to abide by the international rules of the road may be, no one ever said China's transition to full-fledged trading partner would be easy. Lee's board members—just like the rest of China—are grappling with economic and societal changes of mind-boggling proportions, often with little to guide them but the rusty compass of a discredited, dysfunctional socialist system. On the surface, the glassy towers and freshly paved boulevards of China's sprawling cities evoke the 21st century. But, especially when it comes to business practices, the country's modernity can be as thin as the glaze on a Ming Dynasty ceramic. Nevertheless, the WTO ascent "is a historic juncture," says Yu Shen, president of the Shanghai Customs College and one of China's top WTO experts. "It's an opportunity for China to establish itself as a major player in the global economic community. Once you enter the WTO, you enter the world stage, and you must play by the rules."

Rules? Some 900 pages of China's WTO trade pledges have yet to be translated into putonghua, and even that is merely the first step toward bringing the provinces' Byzantine regional and local

---

business laws into compliance. Since entry, the entire country has been gripped with a sense of urgency—a feeling that everything must change overnight. Millions of workers, officials, and other would-be capitalists are struggling to reinvent themselves as business executives who can compete in the global economy. Billboards proclaim the benefits of the WTO. Taxi drivers recite chapter and verse the pros and cons of WTO membership like so many memorized school lessons: access to more modern technology and markets versus the dangers of foreign competition. From talk on the streets of Beijing, you'd think either the country's industries are about to be obliterated, or that the Middle Kingdom is going to be instantly transformed into a world-class economy.

Both scenarios will in all likelihood turn out to be correct. It's just a matter of timing. Many thousands of inefficient state-owned enterprises will lose the protection of state subsidies and will survive only through wrenching restructuring and rapid modernization. Foreigners will be able to compete in Chinese industries, from banking to delivery services to retail, on an equal footing with domestic companies. The WTO will help the central government push forward with some of its more sensitive reforms, allowing bankrupt factories to shut down. Eventually, the transparency required by WTO regulations will promote rule of law, meritocracy and fair play.

But there will be enormous resistance along the way, as entrenched and corrupt local bosses and factory managers fight to hang on to turf. The Communist Party is scheduling study sessions across the country for officials and factory managers to learn the new regulations. Mainlanders are eagerly devouring self-help books such as *What Joining the WTO Gives the Chinese*. Command economy habits, however, will not be swept away by slogans and light reading. In a recent survey of state-owned companies undergoing restructuring, only 59% of those polled said their goal was to increase profitability, compared with some 90% of companies in the U.S., according to human resource consultants Watson Wyatt in Beijing. While government propaganda pressures state-run enterprises to become more efficient, says Jim Leininger of Watson Wyatt, the rank-and-file cling to the familiar culture. When his company probes management structures, exposing the fact that bosses are party hacks or people appointed because of connections, the clients often balk. "They say, 'No, no, we can't touch this,'" says Leininger.

China's entry into the WTO doesn't mean foreign companies, granted a level playing field under the law, will be marching across China like an invading army, either. Many industries, such as telecommunications, securities, insurance, and oil exploration, will remain protected under the agreement. Even in industries that are opening up, there will be roadblocks. In mobile phone networks, for example, China has agreed to allow foreign companies to take 24% equity stakes in networks in Beijing, Shanghai, and Guangzhou.

But according to Duncan Clark, head of telecoms research firm BDA in Beijing, such stakes are impossible because the networks in those cities can't be split off from the rest of the two national networks run by state-owned China Mobile and China Unicom. Telecoms investment regulations have yet to be released. A widely leaked draft last year stated that investors would be required to have assets of $10 billion, limiting the number of players to a few global leaders.

Other so-called nontariff barriers that local officials might erect are impossible to predict. "When it comes to doing business in China, take your MBA books and throw them into the garbage," says Laurence Brahm, a Beijing-based lawyer who has written several books about the Chinese economy. "If you don't have local government on your side, good luck. But in China, there is always a way to negotiate over a cup of tea."

The mainland's notorious disregard for legalities will slow implementation of WTO regulations, too. "There are no rules in China—

"When it comes to doing business in China, take your MBA books and throw them into the garbage."—Laurence Brahm, a Beijing-based lawyer

---

none," says Albert Louie, managing director of Beijing-based risk management consultants Albert William & Associates. The Chinese are adept at finding indirect ways to punish businesses. For example, when the French irritated Beijing with a plan to sell submarines to Taiwan in the early 1990s, officials used tax measures to hit back at French joint ventures in China. "If the Chinese government wants you dead," he says, "they can always do it. This is their home turf."

Local governments have plenty of reason to try to protect their factories—major employers that have formed community backbones for a generation or more. Duo Duo Le Electronic Ltd. in Guangzhou, which used to export 40,000 VCD players a year, is pulling out of the line because of the WTO. Liu Duo, the company's president, figures that once foreign competitors arrive, a survival-of-the-fittest struggle will unfold. Branding will be the key to building sustainable businesses, and he says he can't afford TV commercials. "We can't afford to compete," he says. Instead, Liu is planning to produce electric water heaters, a less competitive commodity.

In some sectors, the sense that barbarians are about to overrun the compound is palpable. "When foreign banks come in, they will take our best employees and our best customers," says Li Ruogu, deputy governor of the People's Bank of China. "Five years is a very short period for our banks to adjust. But we promised, so we must deliver." The government has yet to publish its WTO agreements, in part for fear that the public will be angry that China made too many concessions (the WTO document itself is reportedly under guard around-the-clock). Some predict that China's entry into the WTO will relegate domestic operators to commercial backwaters. "Foreign companies will dominate all the high-margin sectors," says Meng Fancheng, an official with AT Kearney management consultants in Shanghai. "We can only pray for the best."

Notwithstanding the reasonable fears of a country facing sweeping societal shifts, China isn't blindly throwing the gates open to predators. Beijing hopes the rigors of the WTO will instill market discipline. Capital and talent will be attracted, in turn seeding management ranks and setting in motion the forces of modernization. The government is focusing on building favored state-owned enterprises that will dominate each industry. Companies such as Sinochem, Baosteel, China Netcom, and Shanghai Autoworks Industrial Corp., for example, are being groomed by the government and are likely to thrive. Budding entrepreneurs in small, private Chinese companies also relish the opportunities promised by the WTO. Yes, foreign companies will have more room to maneuver, but so will domestic firms. "They don't allow us into sectors such as railroads, steel, telecom operator licenses," says Hu Chenzhong, chairman of Delixi, a private Wenzhou-based maker of electrical power switches. "But, slowly, we will be allowed in."

Beijing's challenge will be managing all the change—and preventing social unrest. Millions of workers will lose their jobs as state enterprises slim down or shut down. WTO may also exacerbate the gaping divide between rich city dwellers and impoverished peasants in the countryside. There's no turning back, however. And as Lee discovered at his recent board meeting, the way forward won't be predictable. China will do what it will. "At the end of the day, you have to learn to do things the Chinese way," says Lee. Crack open those Chinese WTO primers—and develop a taste for tea.

China's Coming Transformation[2]

By George Gilboy and Eric Heginbotham
Foreign Affairs, July/August 2001

The Main Event

Social forces unleashed by China's economic reform over the last 20 years are now driving inexorably toward a fundamental transformation of Chinese politics. Since the suppression of the 1989 student protests in Tiananmen Square, China's leaders have struggled to maintain the political status quo, even while pursuing rapid economic reform. The result today is a nonadaptive, brittle state that is unable to cope with an increasingly organized, complex, and robust society. Further efforts to resist political change will only squander the benefits of social and economic dynamism, perpetuate the government's costly battle to contain the populace, drive politics toward increasingly tense domestic confrontation, and ultimately threaten the system with collapse.

Many of today's senior Chinese officials recognize this dilemma but have powerful personal motivations to resist change. The next generation of Chinese leaders, however—set to take office in 2002–3—is both more supportive of reform and less constrained by Tiananmen-era political baggage. These new leaders will likely respond to the dilemma, therefore, by accelerating political liberalization. This does not imply that China will soon become a Western-style democracy. Rather, the coming steps in reform will likely include measures to legitimize independent social organization, give citizen groups increased input in policymaking (in exchange for some limits on their activities), and develop greater intraparty democracy. These changes will be difficult, and in the near term, they are as likely to throw China into domestic turmoil as they are to create a stable partial democracy.

This coming political reformation is *the* main event in China, and it has critical implications for Sino-U.S. relations. Events such as the recent collision of a U.S. spy plane with a Chinese fighter jet near Hainan Island, the detention of foreign academics in China, or even rhetorical skirmishes across the Taiwan Strait cannot by themselves derail or even significantly delay the forces of change. The event most likely to disrupt the coming reform effort would be the emergence of a clearly adversarial relationship between the United States and China—a new cold war. Such a development

---

2. Article by George Gilboy and Eric Heginbotham from *Foreign Affairs* July/August 2001. Copyright © *Foreign Affairs*. Reprinted with permission.

would reinforce the position of Chinese conservatives and militarists and weaken the forces that are currently driving change. Accordingly, U.S. policy should be restrained and carefully calibrated to maintain regional security while encouraging continued reform and liberalization in China.

Brittle State

China's current leaders view politics through the prism of two central episodes in their political lives: the Cultural Revolution of the mid-1960s and the 1989 Tiananmen Square demonstrations. The Cultural Revolution made today's leaders averse to radicalism and mass action, and the Tiananmen demonstrations made them wary of social and political liberalization. These two experiences have framed the boundaries of "safe" and "stable" politics in China—not too radical, not too liberal.

In the days leading up to the Tiananmen crackdown, the Commu-

---

China's current leaders view politics through the prism of two central episodes in their political lives: the Cultural Revolution of the mid-1960s and the 1989 Tiananmen Square demonstrations.

---

nist Party's senior leaders came to believe that the demonstrations, if left unchecked, could lead to the violent overthrow of party rule and the onset of social chaos. Firmly implanted in their minds was China's vivid history of small gatherings growing into large movements, often followed by violence and unrest. To these leaders, the Tiananmen demonstrations confirmed that limited political dissent could rapidly attract support from other groups seeking to vent their own dissatisfactions. Indeed, the student gatherings in 1989 began not as protests but as spontaneous mourning for the death of the relatively liberal party leader Hu Yaobang. Once gathered, however, the students quickly added calls for accelerated economic and political reform. Senior party leaders were caught off-guard by the students' vehement criticism and swift organization. They were even more alarmed by the other groups that coalesced in support of the students, especially well-organized urban workers. After weeks of demonstrations and fruitless negotiations, the protesters were finally dispersed by the military, at the cost of many lives.

In the years since, China's leaders have shown little tolerance for challenges to their authority. Although Western headlines tend to focus on Beijing's tough stance against public protests, even more important for China's future may be the regime's general intolerance of independent social organization. The government has not

permitted the rise of representative institutions capable of giving
people a feeling of participation or investment in the governing
system. This unwillingness to deal with groups that are not dominated and controlled by the party locks the state in a constant
struggle to hold back a rising tide of self-organizing social and economic entities.

The political rigidity of the current regime stands out when compared to the flexibility of Deng Xiaoping's 1980s leadership. Before
1989, Deng had promoted intraparty democratization, village elections, and the devolution of power to the provinces. He had even
promoted the separation of party and state to reduce the Communist Party's interference in administrative affairs. In contrast, the
current generation of leaders, including President Jiang Zemin,
has eschewed further political and institutional reform in favor of
accelerating economic reform.

Despite the current regime's unwillingness to move forward on
political reform, Chinese politics and society have remained more
stable than most foreign observers predicted in the aftermath of

---

*Today, many Chinese families find
computers, designer clothes, mobile phones,
and home-entertainment centers within their
reach.*

Tiananmen. Since the 1989 uprising, no political dissident movements have been able to inspire similar widespread public support.
This quiescence is not simply attributable to the coercion and suppression of civil society. Over the last ten years, Beijing has sustained its nonadaptive state by scoring a series of economic and
social successes that have appreciably improved the quality of life
for most Chinese.

The most important of these achievements has been increased
material prosperity. According to official statistics, China's annual
real GDP growth averaged 9.7 percent between 1989 and 2000. In
aggregate terms, real urban incomes more than doubled over the
same period. For many Chinese families, the increased prosperity
of the 1990s can be measured by the new range of goods that they
can now afford. The prizes of the 1980s included basic items such
as refrigerators and television sets. Today, many Chinese families
find computers, designer clothes, mobile phones, and home-entertainment centers within their reach as well.

This growing prosperity is the result of the Chinese government's
commitment to structural economic reforms. Measures to legitimize private capital and grant private firms the same legal rights
as state-owned businesses have laid the foundation for sustained,
market-based growth. Today, more than 40 percent of industrial
output comes from private companies, and more than 30 percent of

nonagricultural employees work for private or mixed-ownership firms. (In contrast, virtually no privately owned industrial firms existed in 1979 when Deng's economic reform began.)

Beijing has also achieved greater integration with the global economy. China's international trade has more than quadrupled, from $112 billion in 1989 to $474 billion in 2000, and no other country in the world, besides the United States, receives more foreign direct investment. Between 1996 and 1999, China's FDI totaled $126 billion—more than six times that of Japan. Beijing's commitment to join the World Trade Organization (WTO) will further open the economy to foreign trade, investment, and international supervision.

Along with these economic reforms have come greatly expanded personal liberties. Individual Chinese, especially city-dwellers, are now free to create their own lifestyles: they can move about the country, start their own businesses, and express themselves on a wide range of issues. Those who wish to travel abroad can now obtain passports to do so, provided they have enough money. Even China's controversial one-child policy, often a target of criticism in the West, has been relaxed, first in rural communities and more recently in Shanghai.

> *Armed with greater wealth and liberty, Chinese society has gained a spirited life of its own.*

Jiang's regime has been able to achieve all this while delivering what has been perhaps the most stable decade in the last 150 years of China's tumultuous history. This stability taps into a deep-seated longing among many Chinese to leave behind the misery of past foreign invasions, civil wars, and violent mass political movements. Not only has it provided an environment conducive to economic growth, but it has made most people feel secure that today's newfound wealth can be enjoyed tomorrow.

These achievements have offered both the means and the incentive for new groups to form and organize. But the Chinese leadership, fearful of political dissent and social organization, has been unwilling to adapt politics to new social realities. This reluctance has resulted in a brittle state that is increasingly unable to sustain the social stability and economic growth of the past decade.

Robust Society

Armed with greater wealth and liberty, Chinese society has gained a spirited life of its own, generating a constant stream of both formal and informal organizations. Most of this activity—from labor movements to consumer advocacy to animal-rights activism—is normal and healthy in any market-based economy. But when social dynamism is suppressed, some of its energy is channeled into unhealthy activities, such as violent protest. All of this requires the state to find new ways to understand, mediate between, and govern groups in society. One thing is certain: the regime's current methods of social control will not work.

The state's ability to control and coerce the populace has withered. For example, urban neighborhood committees, one of the regime's key means of monitoring its citizens, have dramatically declined in power and relevance. These committees once dominated life in the pervasive housing tracts run by state-owned companies. Through their connection to the work unit, or *danwei*, they ruled over critical aspects of everyday life, such as housing, employment, and benefits, controlling society at the neighborhood level. But over the past two decades of economic reform, rising incomes, a growing private sector, the contraction of state firms, and the privatization of housing have all conspired to weaken the neighborhood committee system. In the countryside, the decline of collective farming has led to a similar relaxation of state control over the lives of individuals.

A fundamental shift in the balance of power between Chinese state and society is underway.

A fundamental shift in the balance of power between Chinese state and society is underway. With each passing day, the government understands less about its own people, while its power to affect social outcomes wanes. Meanwhile, the number of "actively dissatisfied" groups has grown. In 1989, political dissent was largely limited to activist students, a few reform politicians, and some urban workers. Today, however, new powerful actors have emerged to press for their own interests.

Farmers. With increasing frequency, Chinese farmers are organizing to protest corrupt local officials, onerous and arbitrary taxes, and extreme poverty. In recent months, farmers have attacked tax collectors, blocked roads, and fought with officials and police. In April 2001, for example, more than 600 police and paramilitary troops stormed the southern village of Yuntang, where villagers had barricaded the only road into town and steadfastly refused to pay taxes that they called illegal and unreasonably high.

The unemployed. As economic reform continues, millions of Chinese workers are being laid off each year with little hope of reemployment or adequate social welfare support. In some cities, unemployed workers are now joining together in large-scale protests, involving as many as 20,000 people at a time. Such demonstrations wracked the north-eastern cities of Huludao and Liaoyang in the spring of last year. And similar disturbances now occur almost daily in cities and towns throughout the country.

Consumers. Today's Chinese consumers frequently speak out and organize against defective products, financial scams, and official corruption. When these actions are aimed at state agencies or firms, they highlight the government's conflicts of interest as well as the weakness of economic and regulatory institutions. Consumer dissatisfaction may soon become more apparent in China's ill-regulated domestic stock market, in which the government has been encouraging individual investment. Most Chinese investors interpret this encouragement as government assurance that they will make money, and they are likely to hold the government, not the market, responsible for any major shakeout.

Industry associations. Because China's official industry associations are weak and dominated by the Communist Party, they are unable to mediate effectively between industry and government. Yet some industry leaders have coalesced to force the central government to change policies on taxes, international trade, and price reforms. Still, these groups are neither formal nor transparent to the rest of society. They do not fully represent the collective interests of their sectors, nor are they held accountable for their activities. Private entrepreneurs and even state-enterprise managers are now pressuring the government to grant greater independence to official industry associations or to formally recognize unofficial ones. Ironically, working with democratic, independent industry groups is not unknown in China. The central government (and many local governments) already regularly meet with chambers of commerce and industry associations that represent foreign firms in China, often consulting them on key regulatory and policy issues.

Labor unions. Although China's official labor unions, like its formal industry associations, are dominated by the Communist Party, many of them are now pressing for greater organizational independence. And despite the arrests of many would-be organizers of unofficial unions, attempts to establish new, fully independent labor groups continue. Even foreign firms in China have asked the government to allow the formation of stronger, more representative unions because they believe such groups will help their managers better negotiate with their workers.

Religious and spiritual movements. The rise of the Falun Gong is only the most visible indication of resurgent spiritualism in China. Traditional religions, mystical movements, and cults have attracted millions of followers in recent years. Some observers estimate that 30 million Christians now live in China, about half of them belonging to underground churches. In Beijing alone, the number of unauthorized churches has reportedly grown from 200 in 1996 to around 1,000 today. Despite a recent government crackdown that destroyed hundreds of unsanctioned churches and temples, the state will be hard pressed to keep up with today's ever-quickening pace of spiritual activity.

Special-interest groups. A variety of nascent special-interest groups, ranging from environmental and animal-rights organizations to regional soccer clubs (which are sometimes prone to hooliganism), now place new demands on the state for resources and attention. For example, environmental groups—some with nation-wide reach—have sponsored direct actions such as tree-planting programs and petitions calling for better municipal waste management. Such groups provide important services to society, but their potential for mobilizing people on a regional or even nationwide scale makes the government nervous.

Separatists. Finally, separatist groups continue to challenge the regime's authority directly. Tibetans have long resisted Chinese rule, sometimes with peaceful protest, sometimes with violence. Muslim separatists in the westernmost province of Xinjiang receive training and weapons from Muslim groups in Central Asia and are engaged in armed confrontation with the state. Their most militant elements attack police, soldiers, and other government officials, and the state has responded with equal force. According to estimates from international observers, 210 people were sentenced to death for separatist activities between 1997 and 1999.

It is becoming difficult for the Chinese government to ignore or

---

Coping with China's increasingly organized and informed society is the greatest challenge facing Beijing's next generation of leaders.

---

conceal these social changes. Information on even the most sensitive topics is available from foreign sources across increasingly porous borders, and even China's state-run media have become a regular source of news on many domestic problems. As a result, nearly everyone in China today is aware of the beneficial work of entrepreneurs, consumer groups, and animal-rights activists. They also receive detailed reports about railroad disruptions and factory seizures by disgruntled workers, as well as pervasive corruption among village officials. Increased access to information has helped create a public opinion in China, and the regime already feels obliged to respond.

Rising to the Challenge

Coping with China's increasingly organized and informed society is the greatest challenge facing Beijing's next generation of leaders. The nation's new leaders will seek ways not only to maintain continued economic growth but also to reinvigorate legitimacy and popular support. A key element of this reformation will be greater acceptance of and dialogue with legitimate independent associations. Both state and society would benefit from the success of such efforts. The state would be better able to govern, and society would enjoy greater pluralism and new limits on state intervention.

China's new leaders will likely choose change over retrenchment for three reasons. First, many senior officials already recognize that the task of confronting society is becoming more burdensome and difficult. The stability of the last decade is showing signs of wearing thin. According to a speech attributed to Prime Minister Zhu Rongji, China suffered 117 incidents of armed, violent protest last year. Those incidents resulted in more than 4,300 casualties, of which more than half were party cadres and government officials. In some of these cases, thousands of security personnel were mobilized before order was restored.

Although these protests have not yet reached the size and significance of the 1989 Tiananmen demonstrations, they have been enough to lead some party officials to question Beijing's current inflexibility on social and political issues. For example, several senior provincial police cadres—overwhelmed by their duties to contain the Falun Gong—have reportedly petitioned the leadership to take a more accommodating approach toward the spiritual group. For some business managers, many of whom are also party members, the crackdown and its associated political study sessions have diverted attention from pressing administrative, commercial, and management problems. Indeed, dissent within the party on the Falun Gong issue may run deep: even some top officials may believe that the government's policy has gone too far.

A second incentive for political reform is that the continued suppression of social organization and institution building threatens to hamper economic development. Weak institutions contribute to waste and inefficiency, discourage investment, and limit the prospects for further rapid growth. Foreign firms in China have long complained about the lack of market information, clear regulations, enforceable contracts, and good coordination among suppliers. The costs of these inadequacies are also high for Chinese companies. Weak economic institutions—such as the party-dominated labor unions and industry associations—cannot effectively exchange people and information, pool resources, set standards, present policymakers with unified industry views, or even adequately interact with one another. These shortcomings result in fragmented industries, isolated firms, and poorly informed managers, all of which raise costs and discourage investment in new, productive businesses.

The weakness of economic institutions also threatens to retard the technological learning and innovation that is critical for future productivity gains and economic growth. Innovation is not simply a matter of money, science, or market competition—although all three elements are essential. Innovation also requires close interaction among firms, universities, research and development institutes, and all levels of government. In many of the world's most innovative countries, this interaction often occurs through regional development agencies, industry and professional associations, and sector-specific financial consortia. Yet in China, despite appeals by industrial leaders and even state science and technology officials, the regime's reluctance to accept independent civil society has stifled the development of such organizations. Beijing's Zhongguancun area—often called China's Silicon Valley—has generated little real innovation, largely because it lacks the dense interfirm networks and cooperative business culture that has made America's Silicon Valley so successful.

The third reason that China's new leaders will likely choose change stems from their personal affiliations and career interests. The clear front-runner to replace Jiang is Vice President Hu Jintao, whose political background is in the Communist Youth League, a relatively liberal wing of the party. Even though Hu may not emerge as the primary driver of political reform (and indeed may take a relatively cautious position on that issue), he will likely try to promote an unprecedented number of officials with Youth League and other reform-related backgrounds. This drive may be complemented by the efforts of today's reform-minded leaders (such as Zhu Rongji and Li Ruihuan) to promote their own proteges.

Regardless of who gains which specific posts in the government, powerful political motivations may also drive the new leadership toward reform. In the decade since the Tiananmen Square crisis, many hard-line leaders have passed from the scene, and those that remain have become more vulnerable to major revisions of the verdict on that issue. Accordingly, those untainted by the legacy of Tiananmen are increasingly tempted to leapfrog over their seniors by seizing the banner of reform. This trend has already begun, with the disclosure of the *Tiananmen Papers* and other documents now being smuggled out of China by factions of the Communist Party.

Containing China's Reform?

For China's next generation of leaders, political reform will center on allowing independent social organizations to formally represent their interests, strengthening intraparty democracy, and increasing the separation of the Communist Party from the state. These measures will recast relations between state and society and could be the first steps toward greater political pluralism. The experiences of South Korea, Mexico, and Taiwan demonstrate that a variety of paths can lead from one-party rule toward political liberalization. None of them offers a quick and painless transition to full democracy. Rather, they entail a gradual conciliation with society's new forces and a phased-in introduction of democratic institutions and values.

Nor is success guaranteed. It will be difficult to govern China's huge, powerful, and potentially fractious society during the inevitable disruptions of a major transition. Even if intent on reform, China's new leadership could botch the job. If it does, the China of tomorrow could look more like today's Indonesia or Yugoslavia than South Korea or Taiwan. Whatever the outcome, China is on the cusp of more than just a change in leadership personnel. The coming

> *Even if intent on reform, China's new leadership could botch the job.*

set of reforms is likely to set in motion a process of political change that may be longer and more tumultuous than anyone has yet imagined. Despite these risks, however, it is in the interest of Beijing's next generation to attempt reform. And it is in the interest of the United States to encourage them to do so.

The advent of a new cold war between the United States and China, however, would discourage Beijing's new leaders from pursuing political reform. Explicitly adversarial Sino-U.S. relations would validate Chinese conservatives' arguments about American intentions to weaken China and would leave Chinese liberals open to charges of treason. Moreover, even tomorrow's moderate leaders would be unlikely to run the high risks of reform if they feared the United States might exploit Chinese political divisions. Hence, although the United States needs to defend its legitimate interests in East Asia, it should do so in a restrained manner that provides the least ammunition for reactionary critics in China. In short, Washington should avoid a containment policy that would actually contain China's reform process.

Although dramatic change may still be several years away, moderation and restraint in U.S. policy are needed now. Today's reform-minded leaders are struggling to promote their proteges to key positions in preparation for the coming political transition. The next generation, which will govern China until at least 2008, is still being forged, and specific personnel selections will have a decisive impact on the prospects for reform. It will be difficult, however, for relatively liberal officials to rise to key positions if Sino-U.S. relations descend into cold war.

The United States can take steps to avoid increasing tensions without compromising its core interests. One of the least costly—and most effective—measures is rhetorical moderation. Although suggesting that China could become a "strategic partner" (as the Clinton administration did) was premature but benign, labeling China a "strategic competitor" (as some in the current administration have done) is both premature and pernicious.

The United States should also focus greater attention on the strategic and diplomatic implications of its tactical military activities. Although the U.S. military presence in East Asia generally enhances regional stability, some types of military activities can have adverse effects. China's handling of the recent spy-plane crash near Hainan angered most Americans. Yet American surveillance close to Chinese borders had been conducted at a Cold War level of intensity for a year before the incident occurred. Such U.S. activities may not violate international law, but the intensity and manner in which they have been conducted recently has created an image of a hostile United States without commensurate gains for American security interests.

> *Chinese civilian leaders . . . do not want a new cold war.*

Indeed, a more measured approach to secondary security interests would enhance U.S. leverage on more vital issues, such as halting the proliferation of missiles and weapons of mass destruction (WMD) and encouraging a peaceful resolution of the standoff across the Taiwan Strait. Confrontation could convince China's leaders that WMD proliferation is in their national interest, whereas a firm but more businesslike relationship would help persuade them that it is not. By focusing on core issues, America's voice on them will be amplified.

Chinese civilian leaders, especially those about to take the helm in 2002–3, do not want a new cold war. Confrontation with the United States would jeopardize China's economic reform program and continued prosperity. A cold war would also diminish the civilian leadership's authority relative to that of the military. Having struggled for 20 years to curb the army's role in domestic policy, civilian leaders would be loath to invite the resurgence of military influence that would accompany a descent into cold war.

Moreover, the civilian leadership's ability to use confrontation with the United States to gain popular support for the party is severely limited. Beijing does use historical education to promote the ideas of national unity and past victimization. The government has also permitted the limited expression of social anger immediately following events such as the accidental U.S. bombing of the Chinese embassy in Belgrade. But in all such cases officials have moved quickly to contain domestic passions for fear that even nationalist movements may ultimately threaten the regime itself.

Change is the main event in China, and America should welcome it. Chinese hard-liners will not be able to stop the coming political reform—unless they are aided by an adversarial attitude from the United States. As a great power, the United States can best serve its own interests, as well as those of the Asian region, by behaving with the restraint and grace befitting its status.

China's Challenges[3]

By Peter Hadekel
Gazette (Montreal), May 12, 2001

Since Mao Tse-tung's death 25 years ago, the pace of change in China has been remarkable. This country has become the fastest-growing economy in the world, lifting the living standards of hundreds of millions of its citizens. Its Communist Party rulers have blown up the old model of social and economic conduct and substituted what some like to call *market Leninism*.

But the pace of change has been so rapid that new tensions and strains have been created: economic inequality, a growing thirst for freedom of expression and representative democracy, unrest among ethnic minorities, the collapse of China's social safety net. How China's leaders deal with these pressures will determine its relationship with the rest of the world. As Kevin O'Brien, a China specialist at the University of California at Berkeley, notes, it's hard to imagine just how much this country has changed. As recently as 20 years ago, everyone worked for the government, even in grocery stores and restaurants. There was no such thing as private property. Everyone was assigned a job out of school, lived in apartments allocated by the government and depended on government ration coupons for food. Foreigners lived in compounds protected by armed guards and the Chinese had no contact of any kind with them. A Chinese citizen had no freedom to move about the country and couldn't even buy a train ticket without official permission.

During the last 20 years, personal autonomy has increased dramatically. It's now possible to shop for the widest possible range of consumer goods, to find your own job or start your own business. The Chinese have acquired disposable income and a new class of domestic tourists is visiting the country and booking up all the seats on domestic flights. Mortgages have been introduced and housing bought and sold. Foreign joint ventures have poured hundreds of billions of dollars into new manufacturing plants; Western fashions and pop culture have become the rage.

Iron Grip

At the same time, China's rulers have shown no sign of relaxing their iron grip on dissent. Obsessed by the need to preserve social stability in a land of 1.3 billion people and 55 ethnic minorities, they continue to crack down on anything that smacks of a threat to one-

---

party rule. And they are happy to feed the sense of paranoia that many Chinese people harbour toward the United States. While they like American culture and food, Chinese tend to believe that the United States intentionally bombed the Chinese embassy in Belgrade during the Kosovo war and that the recent mid-air collision between a Chinese fighter and a U.S. surveillance aircraft was a deliberate act on the part of the United States.

So the question becomes: which direction will China now take in the global economy? Will its more open attitude to foreign investment and culture mean that it also will import foreign ideas of representative democracy and relax its sometimes obsessive concern with its own sovereignty?

China's future lies in the hands of the 1,900 students at Shanghai High School, an elite boarding school founded 132 years ago during the Ch'ing dynasty. It is at schools like this that its best and brightest youngsters are trained to become the next generation of leaders.

Vice-Principal Xue Jian-ping proudly boasts of the 70 high-ranking government officials and 30 army generals who are alumni of

---

The country's leaders recognize they cannot divorce themselves from the the Internet age if they want to continue China's economic progress.

---

his school. Admission is limited to those who excel on entrance examinations, and whose families can afford the $500 annual cost. "We encourage our students to experiment, think creatively and come to their own conclusions," Xue says.

In a society that has always tried to discourage independent thinking and that continues to be anchored by the Communist Party, if not by communist ideology, his words invite skepticism. The broader question for Chinese society is whether the experimentation, creativity and independent thinking supposedly encouraged at Shanghai High School can change the direction of a nation and lead to greater individual freedoms.

Stroll through the well-equipped, 320-acre campus of this elite school, with its sports facilities, theatre, music rooms and library, and one gets the sense that change is, indeed, blowing in China. It's 4 p.m. and classes have ended. Students are crammed into the school's computer labs, equipped with about 300 Pentium-3 computers. And they're doing what young people anywhere would do—they're surfing the Net, where they can get relatively unfiltered access to western media.

Obvious Contradictions

The contradictions here are obvious. The country's leaders recognize they cannot divorce themselves from the the Internet age if they want to continue China's economic progress. At the same time, they see the Internet as a threat to their entrenched power. So the government owns and operates China's major Internet portals, just as it still controls the state media.

Even so, you can now get a version of the world on the Web from the U.S. perspective. This is not the 19th century, when imperial China sought to insulate itself from the influence of the foreign traders operating through its treaty ports. At Shanghai High School, vice-principal Xue is quick to point out the school runs a bilingual instruction program stressing excellence in English. A summer camp operated each summer with Harvard University of Cambridge, Mass., gives Chinese students a chance to perfect their English and Americans a chance to improve their Chinese. Presumably, they also talk about rap music.

So let's ask the question again. What kind of China will we see in 10 years? Will the increasing openness to foreign investment, culture and ideas change the rigid thinking at the top? James Liu thinks it will.

Liu is executive vice-president of the Shanghai Stock Exchange, which opened in 1990 and now seeks to dislodge the Hong Kong exchange as the pre-eminent stock market in Asia. "The stock market has played a vital role in reforming the state-owned economy," he says while sipping tea at the striking stock-exchange building in Shanghai's Pudong district.

Even with the enormous strides China has made toward private enterprise, there are still limits on what people can legally claim as their own. "When you buy a house in China, you're really buying a long-term lease from the government," Liu says. "People cannot really own much in this country, but one exception is a share of stock."

Liu sees the ethic of stock ownership as immensely important in reshaping the way the Chinese think about private property. More than 50 million individual investors now participate in the market, and many of them have ridden soaring domestic share prices to overnight riches.

You can glimpse some of them at the Shenyin and Wanguo Securities Ltd. office in downtown Shanghai. Individual investors with at least $60,000 U.S. in their accounts come to the brokerage firm's office each day, log on to a computer and track their share prices. Many of them are women who spend the hours trading gossip and stock tips, playing cards and turning the art of investing into a social occasion.

Liu worries that many of them have no understanding that markets can go down as well as up. He also frets over Shanghai's well-deserved reputation for cowboy capitalism. Several cases of market manipulation and insider trading have hurt the small investor and Liu is now trying to clean up the mess by bringing in foreign expatriates with regulatory experience. Just a few weeks ago, the exchange delisted its first stock, an initial attempt at getting rid of "the bad apples," he says. "It shows we mean business."

Enormous Control

But much more will have to be done if China wants to gain acceptance as a modern economy with transparent rules of behaviour. Despite its capitalist appearance, the truth is that the government still exercises enormous control over the economy. If a company wants to go public, word comes down from the top that the government insists on taking 60 percent of the initial public offering for itself. And so it goes, even when it comes to dealing with multinational giants like General Motors.

The price of admission to China for GM and companies like it is that they have to give 50 percent of the action to the government. At GM's Shanghai plant, opened in 1997, the joint venture partner is a state-owned enterprise.

While GM's experience has been trouble-free, sometimes, such marriages can end in trouble. If a dispute between the joint-venture partners arises, there's not much in the way of rule of law to settle the issue. Corruption, endemic in China at the lower levels of bureaucracy, often comes into play.

At the China headquarters of the 3M Company, managing director Kenneth Yu says: "At times, it's been hinted to our sales people that if they could do a little more (for a government official) they could get more. But we walk away from anything that looks like a gray area."

Once China joins the World Trade Organization, an even brighter light will be shined on these practices. WTO membership, too, will mean many people will be cut loose from uncompetitive state-supported enterprises. Massive layoffs in a country that already has a population of homeless migrant workers estimated at 130 million will pose huge risks for the country's stability and huge challenges for the next head of the Chinese state.

It's a Fascist Regime[4]

BY MICHAEL A. LEDEEN
NATIONAL POST, FEBRUARY 23, 2002

As President Bush, now in Beijing, gets up close to the rulers of China, he must have conflicting feelings.

We are told that the Chinese have helped us fight terror, which is cause for satisfaction. On the other hand, the CIA has recently revised sharply upwards its estimate of Chinese military power in the near future, which is cause for concern. As he ponders what China is and may be, Mr. Bush might reflect that the People's Republic is something quite unique, and therefore very difficult to understand.

China is not, as is invariably said, in transition from communism to a freer and more democratic state. It is, instead, something we have never seen before: a maturing fascist regime. This new phenomenon is hard to recognize, both because Chinese leaders continue to call themselves communists, and also because the fascist states of the first half of the 20th century were young, governed by charismatic and revolutionary leaders, and destroyed in World War II. China is anything but young, and it is governed by a third or fourth generation of leaders who are anything but charismatic. The current and past generations of Chinese leaders, from Deng Xiaoping to Jiang Zemin, may have scrapped the communist economic system, but they have not embraced capitalism. To be sure, the state no longer owns "the means of production." There is now private property, and, early last June, businessmen were formally admitted to the Communist Party. Profit is no longer taboo; it is actively encouraged at all levels of Chinese society, in public and private sectors. And the state is fully engaged in business enterprise, from the vast corporations owned wholly or in part by the armed forces, to others with top management and large shareholders simultaneously holding government jobs.

This is neither socialism nor capitalism; it is the infamous "third way" of the corporate state, first institutionalized in the 1920s by the founder of fascism, Benito Mussolini, then copied by other fascists in Europe.

Like the earlier fascist regimes, China ruthlessly maintains a single-party dictatorship; and although there is greater diversity of opinion in public discourse and in the media than there was a generation ago, there is very little wiggle room for critics of the system, and no toleration of advocates of Western-style freedom and democ-

---

racy. Like the early fascist regimes, China uses nationalism—not the standard communist slogans of "proletarian international-ism"—to rally the masses. And, like the early fascisms, the rulers of the People's Republic insist that virtue consists in sublimating individual interests to the greater good of the nation. Indeed, as we have seen recently in the intimidation and incarceration of over-seas Chinese, the regime asserts its right to dominate all Chinese, everywhere. China's leaders believe they command a people, not merely a geographic entity.

Unlike communist leaders, who extirpated traditional culture and replaced it with a sterile Marxist-Leninism, the Chinese enthusiastically mine the millennia of Chinese thought to provide legitimacy for their own actions. No socialist realism here! Indeed, this open embrace of ancient Chinese culture is one of the things that has most entranced Western observers. Many believe that a country with such ancient roots will inevitably demonstrate its profound humanity in social and political practice. Yet the fascist leaders of the 1920s and '30s did the same. Mussolini rebuilt Rome

---

Like the early fascisms, the rulers of the People's Republic insist that virtue consists in sublimating individual interests to the greater good of the nation.

---

to provide a dramatic visual reminder of ancient glory, and Hitler's favorite architect built neoclassical buildings throughout the Third Reich.

Like their European predecessors, the Chinese claim a major role in the world because of their history and culture, not because of their current power, or scientific or cultural accomplishments. Just like Germany and Italy in the interwar period, China feels betrayed and humiliated, and seeks to avenge historic wounds. China even toys with some of the more bizarre notions of the ear-lier fascisms, like the program to make the country self-sufficient in wheat production—the same quest for "autarky" that obsessed both Hitler and Mussolini.

It is therefore wrong to think of contemporary China as an intensely unstable system, riven by the democratic impulses of capitalism on the one hand, and the repressive instincts of commu-nism on the other. Fascism may well have been a potentially stable system, despite the frenzied energies of Hitler's Germany and Mussolini's Italy. After all, fascism did not fall as the result of internal crisis; it was destroyed by superior force of arms. Fascism was alarmingly popular; Hitler and Mussolini swept to power atop genuine mass movements, and neither Italians nor Germans pro-duced more than token resistance until the war began to be lost.

Since classical fascism had such a brief lifespan, it is hard to know whether or not a stable, durable fascist state is possible. Economically, the corporate state may prove more flexible and adaptable than the rigid central planning that doomed communism in the Soviet empire and elsewhere (although the travails of Japan, which also tried to combine capitalist enterprise with government guidance, show the kinds of problems China will likely face). And our brief experience with fascism also makes it difficult to evaluate the possibilities of political evolution.

Although Hitler liked to speak of himself as primus inter pares, the first among racial equals, he would not have contemplated the democratization of the Third Reich, nor would Mussolini have yielded power to the freely-expressed will of the Italian people. It seems unlikely that the leaders of the People's Republic will be willing to make such a change either. If they were, they would not be so palpably concerned that the Chinese people might seek to emulate the democratic transformation of Taiwan.

To be sure, the past is not a reliable guide to the future. China has already amazed the world with its ability to transform itself in record time. Many scholars believe that China's entry into the World Trade Organization will bring further dramatic change, as the Chinese have to cope with freer competition and a greatly enhanced foreign presence. They may be right, but I have doubts. For the most part, politics trumps economics when the survival of a powerful regime is at stake, and the Chinese leaders have often said they have no intention of following Mikhail Gorbachev's example.

Meanwhile, Mr. Bush has to contend with the present state of affairs, and must evaluate the risks and challenges of contemporary China. Classical fascism was the product of war, and its leaders praised military virtues and embarked upon military expansion. Chinese leaders often proclaim a peaceful intent, yet they are clearly preparing for war, and have been for many years. Optimists insist that China is not expansionist, but optimists pooh-poohed Hitler's imperialist speeches too, and there is a lot of Chinese rhetoric that stresses Beijing's historic role, as if there were an historic entitlement to superpower status.

Thus, classical fascism should be the starting point for our efforts to understand the People's Republic. Imagine Italy 50 years after the Fascist revolution, Mussolini dead and buried, the corporate state intact, the party still firmly in control, the nation governed by professional politicians and a corrupt elite rather than the true believers. No longer a system based on charisma, but on political repression, cynical not idealistic, and formulaic appeals to the grandeur of the "great Italian people," endlessly summoned to emulate the greatness of its ancestors.

That is China today. It may be with us quite a while.

China Looks to the Future[5]

By David R. Sands
Washington Times, April 28, 2002

It was classic Hu Jintao—making his point while preserving his options. In 1999, Chinese Prime Minister Jiang Zemin received a letter from a student at Beijing University accusing one of the school's lecturers of promoting "bourgeois liberalism," a transgression that had provoked divisive ideological fights and destroyed several careers in the mid-1980s. Mr. Jiang ordered Mr. Hu, whose collection of top Communist Party and government posts includes the party's top office for ideological correctness, to handle the matter.

Mr. Hu's Solomonic solution: He ordered party propagandists to produce essays criticizing bourgeois liberalism but put a sharp limit on the number produced and decreed they would only be published by one national newspaper.

It was, noted a well-connected Chinese political analyst who writes under the pen name Yao Jin, one more case in a long career in which Mr. Hu took on thankless jobs and managed to "patch up the quarrel in a way acceptable to both the conservative and reformist wings of the party."

Vice President Hu Jintao, the man in line to become leader of the world's most populous country for perhaps the next decade, faces one of his biggest tests this week as he travels to Washington for the first time to meet with President Bush and Vice President Richard B. Cheney.

The meetings come at yet another bumpy time in relations between Washington and Beijing, with Taiwan, human rights and China's record on weapons proliferation topping a long list of irritants between the two countries.

Mr. Hu arrived in Honolulu yesterday, his first-ever visit to the United States and the first stop on a four-city tour that will take him to San Francisco, New York (where he will visit the site of the September 11 attacks on the World Trade Center) and to Washington.

"My current visit is aimed at implementing the consensus reached at the talks between President Jiang Zemin and President Bush in Beijing, strengthening the high-level contact between China and the United States, enhancing mutual understanding and pushing forward the Sino-U.S. constructive and cooperative relationship," Mr. Hu said in a statement in Honolulu.

---

5. Article by David R. Sands from the *Washington Times* April 28, 2002. Copyright © 2002 News World Communications, Inc. Reprinted with permission of the *Washington Times*.

"May the friendship between the Chinese and American people last forever," he said.

Mr. Hu, who is set to be confirmed as Communist Party chief this fall and to take over as prime minister in March, comes to Washington at the invitation of Mr. Cheney. He will meet Mr. Bush and also attend a working dinner with Secretary of State Colin L. Powell.

> *Mr. Hu is "Jiang's successor, not his choice."*—Joseph Fewsmith, Boston University

His only public appearance here is a dinner hosted by the National Committee on U.S.-China Relations, where he is expected to give an address on Sino-U.S. ties.

Few expect any substantive breakthroughs during Mr. Hu's visit, but U.S. officials and private China-watchers are hungry for more clues to the enigmatic 59-year-old Mr. Hu, who despite a cautious and colorless public style has fashioned an unprecedentedly swift climb through the Chinese political echelon.

He made it to the top despite not being the first choice of his nominal boss, Mr. Jiang, who favored a rival candidate and could prove a behind-the-scenes headache for Mr. Hu even after relinquishing his major posts by next year.

Mr. Hu is "Jiang's successor, not his choice," observed Joseph Fewsmith, an expert on Chinese politics at Boston University's Department of International Relations.

"Who's Hu" in China

The fact that Mr. Hu, a hydraulic engineer by training, has thrived in the treacherous upper rungs of the Chinese Communist Party has inspired a virtual cottage industry of "Who's Hu?" speculation among China watchers on the sources of his influence and longevity.

With China facing major foreign-policy challenges as well as massive economic and social dislocation as it joins the World Trade Organization (WTO), the talents and political leanings of Mr. Hu and other members of the rising "fourth generation" of Chinese Communist leaders will shape the country for years to come.

Said John Tkacik, a onetime Foreign Service officer in China and now a research fellow at the Heritage Foundation, "No Chinese Communist since the early days of the party has risen so far, so fast, and stayed there despite the lack of a strong power base."

Suisheng Zhao, executive director of the University of Denver's Center for U.S.-China Cooperation and editor of the *Journal of Contemporary China*, said Mr. Hu faces a "very delicate task" in Washington, particularly with Mr. Jiang planning his own valedictory trip here in the fall.

Mr. Hu made no missteps but left few strong impressions during a four-nation tour of Western Europe last fall. The Washington trip is designed to build up his stature as a statesman back home while not upstaging the man who remains his boss.

"They will be watching very carefully back home," Mr. Zhao said. "It's already a sensitive time because of the Taiwan issue, and this trip for Hu can't be a failure but it also can't be too successful."

> *"In all his public remarks, Hu has cautiously toed the party line."*—Yao Jin, **Chinese analyst**

Yao Jin, the pseudonymous Chinese analyst, said Mr. Hu's career recalled the old Chinese proverb: "The bird that sticks its head out gets shot."

"In all his public remarks, Hu has cautiously toed the party line, and no outsiders know where he really stands on economic and political reform and many other critical issues that confront China today," Yao Jin wrote. "His reputation as a political enigma reflects not only a cautious personality but also the pressures on him not to make mistakes and not to upstage Jiang."

The question marks hanging over Mr. Hu are all the more remarkable because he has complied a long track record, linked himself to numerous mentors, and been involved in many of the most contentious political issues of the past two decades.

New Political Figure

He has been the target of international scrutiny at least since 1988 for his role in the violent crackdown on demonstrators while serving as party secretary for Tibet.

Mr. Hu has been his generation's leading political figure at least since 1992, when no less a figure that General Secretary Deng Xiaoping tapped the largely unknown Mr. Hu to organize the critical 14th Communist Party Congress, the gathering that confirmed Mr. Jiang's own rise to power.

By October 1992, Mr. Jiang was securely in charge, and Mr. Hu had become the youngest member of the seven-member Politburo Standing Committee, bypassing dozens of more senior and more prominent party officials.

Boston University's Mr. Fewsmith noted that Mr. Hu has managed to hold on to what has historically been one of the world's most notorious dead-end jobs: No. 2 in the Chinese hierarchy.

If Mr. Hu can obtain and hold on to power over the next five-year term, he will have managed a feat that eluded previous Communist Party heirs apparent in a line from Liu Shaoqi—purged during Mao Tse-tung's Cultural Revolution of the 1960s—to Zhao Ziyang, who lost his post for failing to back the bloody crackdown on democracy activists in Tiananmen Square in 1989.

The problem, China watchers say, is that Mr. Hu's record can be used to support virtually any interpretation, from the unimaginative party functionary (his nickname among Beijing liberalizers is "the grandson," slang for a sycophantic yes-man) to hard-line reactionary to closet anti-corruption reformer.

The benign Mr. Hu is a pragmatic technocrat with little patience for tedious fights over orthodoxy. Among China's urban-oriented leadership, he has an unmatched familiarity with the country's struggling rural poor from his early assignments as an engineer and party official in Gansu and Guizhou, two of the country's most impoverished and desolate regions.

The Right Credentials

He burnished his reformist credentials through his close identification with the Communist Party's Central Party School, which has become an unlikely center of political innovation in recent years, introducing up-and-coming party cadres to Western management concepts and liberalizing political and economic trends.

He has managed to impress a series of mentors across the Chinese political spectrum, from the conservative Song Ping, his first boss in Gansu, to the liberal Hu Yaobang, himself a onetime heir apparent before being swept aside in 1987.

Mr. Hu is a master at putting out internal fires in the hierarchy, and made sure to seat himself at the speaker's table in January, when Deputy Prime Minister Qian Qichen announced a softening on China's policy on contacts with members of Taiwan's governing party.

But there is also plenty of ammunition in Mr. Hu's record for pessimists.

It was Mr. Hu, for example, who was selected by party leaders to read a scathing condemnation of the United States and NATO on national television after an alliance bomb destroyed the Chinese Embassy in Belgrade during the 1999 war in Kosovo.

While Mr. Hu held a cordial get-acquainted meeting during President Bush's visit to Beijing in February, his occasional comments on U.S. policies over the past decade "are riddled with suspicion, if not downright paranoia," noted Heritage's Mr. Tkacik.

In a 1994 speech, Mr. Hu said the United States was pursuing a "global hegemonist strategy," with China as its main rival.

"Interfering in China, subverting China and strangling China's development are strategic principles pursued by the United States," he said.

He has only a thin background in economics, at a time when bloated state enterprises, labor unrest, and the accession of China to the WTO loom as the government's biggest domestic challenges of the coming decade.

Most worrying, Mr. Hu has backed ruthless measures in the past to control dissent. While serving as provincial party leader in Tibet in 1989, Mr. Hu was one of the first regional officials to congratulate the central leadership in Beijing for its suppression of the Tiananmen Square protests.

Crackdown in Tibet

Mr. Hu's rocky tenure in Tibet encapsulates many of the contradictions Western diplomats and analysts see in him.

"There is no doubt that during his time in Lhasa we saw some of the most draconian steps taken against the people of Tibet," said John Ackerly, president of the International Campaign for Tibet. "There was a general crackdown, shooting of unarmed protesters and horrifying accounts of torture of political prisoners."

Mr. Hu was confronted with a difficult situation from the start: Rioting rocked Lhasa, the capital city, the day after his appointment was announced on Dec. 9, 1988.

Mr. Hu's rocky tenure in Tibet encapsulates many of the contradictions Western diplomats and analysts see in him.

Mr. Hu made some early gestures to Tibetan Buddhist leaders, but local unrest continued, fueled by the suspicious death of in January 1989 of the revered religious leader the Panchen Lama.

With reports that leadership in Beijing is divided, Mr. Hu in March imposed martial law on the province and ordered a military crackdown that resulted in the deaths of from 40 to 130 Tibetan protesters.

It is reported that Mr. Hu's decisiveness reportedly won him the approval of Deng Xiaoping, and, with a suspiciously convenient case of altitude sickness, the 47-year-old Mr. Hu was soon on his way to Beijing to begin a rapid climb up the political hierarchy.

Debates continue on whether Mr. Hu acted in Tibet of his own accord or was simply carrying out the orders of his party superiors. Tibetan activists like Mr. Ackerly say they are not ready to write Mr. Hu off.

While Mr. Hu routinely mouths the central government line condemning the "separatist Dalai Lama clique," he has avoided the bitter attacks other Chinese leaders have trained on Tibetan leaders.

"We don't expect Tibet to be one of the first things he would want to tackle as premier, and certainly he took a very hard-line stance," Mr. Ackerly said.

Bush and Lhasa

"But on the other hand, he's the first Chinese leader in a long time with first-hand experience with Tibet and minority issues in the poorer provinces," he said. "If he wants to make a break with the past, he has the credibility to do it."

T. Kumar, advocacy director for Asian affairs at Amnesty International, said it was imperative for Bush administration officials to stress issues such as Tibet, the rule of law and human rights at this week's meeting with Mr. Hu.

"Both sides are trying to make an impression," said Mr. Kumar. "The bottom line is that this guy can make a major change in China's human rights record if he wants to, and the U.S. government should let him know how important the question will be in the relationship."

The Bush administration, according to government sources, is apparently sending a signal of its own. Paula Dobriansky, undersecretary of state for global affairs and the State Department's lead official on Tibet, is expected to be seated next to Mr. Hu at the working dinner this week.

II. The State of the People's Republic

Editor's Introduction

Section two examines domestic matters in China by considering issues related to the economy, education, health care, the media, and the plight of orphans. An article from *Asia Pulse* reports that the Chinese economy grew rapidly in 2001, with the gross domestic product (GNP) increasing by 7.3 percent from the previous year. Despite the strong economy, many Chinese workers fear losing their jobs, as Dexter Roberts, Bruce Einhorn, and Frederik Balfour assert in their article for *Business Week*. Disillusioned by inefficient government policies and job losses caused by corruption and mismanagement by factory managers, millions of Chinese workers have staged public protests. Mobs of angry employees have taken over factories and clashed with police. Although the authorities have been able to control the protests and prevent the workers from organizing on a national scale, the writers predict that the demonstrations will continue until "China's leaders figure out how to give their workers a peaceful way to raise their complaints."

Another dimension to China's economic woes is the widening gap between the rich and the poor, which, according to Michael Dorgan in *Knight-Ridder/Tribune Business News*, has caused a substantial increase in crime in recent years. The strong economy has failed to benefit many of China's poor who, lacking opportunities, turn to crime in order to survive. For Dorgan, this condition is exemplified in the plight of millions of farmers who, after migrating to the city, turn criminal because they fail to find work or can obtain only the lowest-paying jobs. Dorgan adds that most of these crimes go unpunished because China's courts, prosecutors, and police are poorly trained and overworked.

Jiang Xueqin next discusses the state of higher education in China in an article from *The Chronicle of Higher Education*. During the 1990s, the government began allowing students to decide their own career paths and cutting subsidies to the universities. In 1999, when many universities in China began charging tuition for the first time since the Communist revolution in 1949, many poor families could not afford the costs. Jiang explains how, although the newly created student loan program was designed to help poor students, it has actually benefitted wealthier students while excluding those who need it the most.

In the *Far Eastern Economic Review*, Susan V. Lawrence explores the difficulties that so many Chinese have affording health care. Lawrence writes that "the fastest road to poverty in China today is a visit to the doctor—especially in the countryside," where, she asserts, many people do not have access to quality health services. Those who do manage to see a doctor or visit a hospital find themselves burdened with large medical bills. Although President

35

Jiang established a health insurance system for people in rural areas in 2002, Lawrence reports that many people are skeptical of the government's initiative because they are unsure of how it will be funded.

In the next article, from *The Northern Echo*, Christen Pears writes that about 1 million babies, many of them girls, are abandoned each year in China. Many of them die from exposure, while those old enough to walk and talk are picked up by street gangs and used for professional begging. The rest are sent to state-run orphanages, many of which provide low-quality care in miserable conditions. Although adoption by a Western family provides the best hope for orphans, Pears notes that the adoption process in China is tightly controlled by the state, and that many children with disabilities are never adopted.

The final article in this section, by Karl Schoenberger from the San Jose *Mercury News*, looks at Hong Kong five years after its administration was transferred from the United Kingdom to China. Under the terms of the transfer agreement, China agreed to respect civil liberties and the free market in Hong Kong. Nevertheless, Schoenberger writes, many Hong Kong residents are dissatisfied with Chinese rule and disillusioned with the territory's administration, especially since Hong Kong's economy has lagged and its real estate market has crashed.

China Maintains Steady, Rapid Economic Growth in 2001[1]

ASIA PULSE, MARCH 6, 2002

China's economy continued to grow rapidly with good performance and low inflation with the GDP hitting 9.5933 trillion yuan (U.S.$116 billion) in 2001, an increase of 7.3 percent over the previous year, Zeng Peiyan, minister in charge of the State Development Planning Commission, said.

Zeng made the remark on March 6 in his *Report on the Implementation of the 2001 Plan for National Economic and Social Development and on the Draft 2002 Plan for National Economic and Social Development*, to the second plenary meeting of the Fifth Session of the Ninth National People's Congress (NPC).

Fixed-asset investment in the country totaled 3.6898 trillion yuan, up by 12.1 percent. Market prices were stable and the consumer price level rose by 0.7 percent. Imports and exports totaled U.S.$509.8 billion, an increase of 7.5 percent, according to Zeng. Government revenue grew rapidly. The financial deficit was kept below the budgeted figure. The financial situation remained stable. The net amount of cash put into circulation amounted to 103.6 billion yuan. The balance of international payments was satisfactory and China's foreign reserves totaled U.S.$212.2 billion at the end of 2001. The registered unemployment rate in cities and towns was 3.6 percent. The natural population growth rate was held at 0.695 percent.

The successful convocation of the Ninth APEC Economic Leaders Meeting and other major international conferences in China, the country's accession to the World Trade Organization and Beijing's successful bid to host the 2008 Olympic Games are all indicators that China has further raised its international position and expanded its influence in international affairs.

In general, targets set in the 2001 plan for national economic and social development were basically met, and implementation of the Tenth Five-Year Plan got off to a good start, Zeng Peiyan said. The minister then gave a detailed account of the country's economic conditions in 2001.

The proactive fiscal policy and the prudent monetary policy were continued, with treasury bonds playing an important role in promoting economic and social development. A total of 150 billion yuan worth of long-term treasury bonds was issued in 2001 as

---

approved at the Fourth Session of the Ninth NPC. The investment in projects financed through treasury bonds totaled approximately three trillion yuan. This played a vital role in boosting economic growth, improving the economic structure, increasing employment, improving the people's living standards and enhancing the quality of bank assets.

Industrial restructuring was vigorously promoted, resulting in improved economic growth and better performance of the national economy. The distribution of agriculture continued to improve as production of major crops was gradually concentrated in areas with the best conditions. Fresh progress was made in industrial restructuring. High-tech industries developed rapidly and the electronic information industry grew by 28 percent. Total profits of state-owned and large non-state industrial enterprises hit 465.7 billion yuan, a rise of 8.1 percent.

Incomes of urban and rural residents continued to grow and the people's standard of living improved steadily.

Reforms related to the reform of state-owned enterprises continued to deepen and the institutional environment for economic and social development improved. The reform to introduce the shareholding system in state-owned enterprises was gradually standardized, and efforts were intensified to reform and reorganize enterprises that were performing poorly. Progress was made in reform of the management system in monopoly industries, with reform plans for telecommunications, power and civil aviation completed and inaugurated. Initial steps were taken to set up a system open to the participation of all sectors to provide credit and financial guarantees, mainly for small and medium enterprises.

Establishment of a social security system was accelerated.

There were initial results in rectifying and standardizing market order due to efforts to implement temporary solutions while seeking permanent solutions and focusing on the most crucial problems. The work was concentrated on the fight against smuggling, production and marketing of fake and shoddy goods, fraudulent export tax rebates, evasion of foreign exchange repayment, obtaining foreign exchange under false pretenses and other special cases.

Vigorous efforts were made to develop a more open economy, creating more space for economic growth. Despite an unfavorable international trade environment, the total volume of imports increased by 6.8 percent and exports by 8.2 percent. Imports of advanced technology and key equipment urgently needed domestically and raw and semi-finished materials in short supply continued to grow rapidly. Foreign direct investment in 2001 amounted to U.S.$46.8 billion, a record high and an increase of 14.9 percent. Foreign investment in integrated circuits, computers, telecommunications products and other high-tech projects increased and the number of large projects financed by multinational corporations grew.

More steps were taken in the program to extensively develop the western region with improvements in planning and policy. Fixed-asset investment in the western region increased by 19.3 percent, six percentage points higher than in the eastern region, and in the central region, by 16.3 percent, three percentage points higher. A number of major projects were also launched last year.

Unremitting efforts were made to invigorate the country through science, technology and education and maintain sustainable development, with comprehensive progress in all social undertakings. Chinese scientists made breakthrough in human genome, working draft and database for rice genome and super server. With more investment in education, the number of students studying at colleges and universities has more than doubled since the policy of recruiting more students was introduced in 1999. Ecological improvement and environmental protection were intensified. Development of culture, art, the press, publishing, radio, film, TV, social sciences, family planning, health, sports, preservation of cultural and historical relics and other undertakings was accelerated. Radio coverage reached 92.9 percent of the population and TV coverage, 94.1 percent.

Incomes of urban and rural residents continued to grow and the people's standard of living improved steadily. Retail sales of consumer goods totaled 3.7595 trillion yuan, an increase of 10.1 percent over the previous year. Tourism income totaled 499.5 billion yuan, an increase of 10.5 percent. Per capita disposable income of urban residents rose by 8.5 percent and per capita net income of rural residents increased by 4.2 percent.

While noting these achievements, Zeng Peiyan said there exist some problems in social and economic activities. The foundation for rural income growth is far from solid. Much remains to be done by quite a number of state-owned enterprises in terms of internal reform, operating mechanisms, technological progress and modern management. Unemployment pressure and the pressure on the social security system have increased. The deflationary tendency has yet to be completely eliminated. The internal mechanism for state-owned enterprises to increase their fixed-asset investment and the policy environment for non-state investment need to be improved. Investment in science, technology and education and the pattern of trained and qualified personnel cannot meet the needs of economic development. Ecological environmental problems remain outstanding. There are many uncertainties affecting export increase. Market order remains somewhat chaotic.

China's Angry Workers[2]

By Dexter Roberts, Bruce Einhorn, and Frederik Balfour
Business Week, April 8, 2002

Four and a half months ago, the rundown Ferro Alloy Factory shut its doors after a half-century of cranking out metal plates for industry in the grim Chinese city of Liaoyang. When the state-owned enterprise closed, 5,000 people lost their jobs. The workers, accustomed to cradle-to-grave security, were promised pensions and back wages for the previous year. But little or nothing materialized. Meanwhile, say workers, their erstwhile bosses busied themselves selling off factory equipment and pocketing the cash.

The workers were outraged. So, every day for the past few weeks, they have marched through Liaoyang, finishing up on Democracy Road outside the factory, not far from City Hall, where a sign exhorts each passerby to be a "civilized citizen." There, the protesters—often joined by workers from other local factories—noisily demand the money owed them and the arrest of their former bosses. One typical worker—let's call him Li Feng—is owed $240 in back wages, enough to keep him and his family going for four months. For now Li, 55, has a job shoveling coal into a city furnace—but that will end when the weather warms up. None of this sits well with Li's wife, a retired hand at a paper factory. So she has joined the protests. "Life is so hard" for the common people, she says. "But the officials—their salaries keep rising." Angry workers in the streets: It is the Chinese government's gravest challenge. In recent weeks, a rash of protests have erupted in cities throughout the northeast, including Liaoyang, Fushun, and Daqing. In the latter city, thousands have laid siege to a petroleum installation belonging to China's biggest oil company, PetroChina. But the protests are not confined to the industrial centers. At any moment, countless smaller rallies are going on across China, from southwestern Sichuan province to southern Jiangxi province, where farmers are agitating against oppressive taxes and shrinking incomes. Time and again, the government has managed to quell protests with a combination of force and offers of compensation. This latest round of demonstrations, while garnering international attention for their scale and intensity, may end no differently. And while many foreign investors have contingency plans, most remain optimistic. The unrest, says Michael Dell, CEO of Dell Computer Corp, "hasn't deterred us from moving forward. We [understand] the risk."

Still, time is not on Beijing's side. The government can't afford perpetual welfare payments for the Rust Belt's unemployed and disaffected workers, many of whom are only in their 40s and see no prospect of new employment in their home provinces. And the pattern of factory shutdowns and layoffs will only accelerate now that China is a member of the World Trade Organization and its decrepit industrial sector must go head-to-head with foreign competition. "This is the No. 1 challenge for China's next generation of leaders," says Hu Angang, a scholar at the Chinese Academy of Sciences, an official think tank. "No country in the world has ever cut so many jobs before."

With workers besieging government offices, blocking roads, and clashing with police, China's formidable state security apparatus is doing everything in its power to prevent the scattered protesters from coming together and forming so much as the seed of a national labor movement. So far, Beijing has managed to contain the situation, thanks to plainclothes police who loiter on every other street corner in strife-torn cities like Liaoyang. Whenever workers try to form independent trade unions, they are immediately crushed. And when the protests get too large, the cops lock the organizers up.

Ultimately, such tactics fan the flames by denying workers the right to protest and negotiate for better deals. "The problems are not economic," says Arthur Waldron, director of Asian studies at the University of Pennsylvania. "It's a political problem. They have to let citizens be citizens. Not letting them be citizens—this is a potentially explosive situation."

Besides, in many cases, the authorities chop the head off the protest movement only to see it grow another. "If you suppress everything," says Nicolas Becquelin, a Hong Kong-based researcher at Human Rights in China, a New York group, "then it's a time bomb."

To defuse it, the government of President Jiang Zemin and Premier Zhu Rongji—which is in its last year of power—is trying to move faster on the policy front. Already Beijing is opening such sectors as tourism, telecoms, and heavy industry to foreign investment. The hope is that foreign companies will soak up many of the jobless and teach them new skills. But many of these initiatives are happening in the southern coastal provinces, where people are richer and have fewer grievances. Crucial for the northeast, a region of ramshackle factories and millions of unemployed, is the creation of a social safety net to help workers absorb the pain as the shakeout accelerates.

This challenge to Beijing's grip on power began about five years ago. That was when China started in earnest to reform the industrial enterprises of its once-proud workshop cities, weaning them off massive subsidies, merging and shuttering factories, and laying off millions. The mass firings were a profound shock for workers who had expected jobs for life. "Ironically, the places that have

A Thousand Protests Blooming

Since Tiananmen, the government has faced rising discontent.

June 4, 1989: Protesting students in Tiananmen Square call for an end to official corruption. Army sent in, killing hundreds, perhaps thousands.

July, 1997: 4,000 silk workers in Mianyang, Sichuan, demonstrate outside city government offices when their factories are closed.

December, 1998: Labor activist Zhang Shangguang sentenced to 10 years in prison in Huaihua, Hunan, for "endangering state security."

December, 1999: 1,000 miners block a railway in Shaanxi over delayed pay; 2,000 retired steelworkers barricade a road in Chongqing after their pensions are slashed.

July, 2000: More than 10,000 farmers riot in Yuandu, Jiangxi, over oppressive taxes and surround government offices.

August: Fearful of losing their jobs, workers in a Tianjin joint venture company take three expatriate managers hostage, including one American, for several days.

December: Thousands of factory workers in Wuhan, Hubei, and Chongqing block city streets and demand unemployment benefits.

April, 2001: A three-year dispute in the village of Yuntang, Jiangxi, over excessive taxation, ends violently when People's Armed Police open fire, killing two farmers and wounding at least 17.

March, 2002: Tens of thousands of factory workers surround government buildings in the northeastern cities of Daqing, Fushun, and Liaoyang, demanding that city officials resign over unpaid unemployment benefits and back pay.

fared the worst are the ones so favored under the planned economy," says Shaomin Li, a marketing professor at City University of Hong Kong. Before long, protests broke out. A turning point came in 1997, when 4,000 workers from a closed silk factory in Sichuan surrounded government offices and demanded unemployment benefits.

As China's market reforms took hold, unemployment went through the roof. While official figures put the urban jobless rate at 3.6%, economists believe it is closer to 15%. In Rust Belt cities the number is more like 25%—a situation that is expected to worsen. According to scholar Hu, over the next few years 10 million workers will be furloughed annually, while an extra 7 million will join the workforce. "It's very difficult to find work for China's people," he says. "Premier Zhu doesn't have an easy job."

Protests are forcing Beijing to slow industrial restructuring. Take the effort to merge Liaoning province's four biggest steel-makers. The plan could make a third of the four companies' 200,000 workers redundant. Now consolidation is impossible. "It is so hard to cut employees," says Liu Zhijiang, an official with the Fushun Iron & Steel Group. "As a state enterprise, we have a responsibility to keep social stability."

With tensions rising, Beijing is resorting to heavy-handed tactics. Police have rounded up four protest leaders in Liaoyang. One, Yao Fuxin, was arrested following a March 17 meeting with city officials to discuss the protesters' grievances. A second man, Xiao Yunliang, was taken into custody two days later; his daughter has heard that he has started a hunger strike to protest his imprisonment. "We don't know what is going to happen to him," she says. "We don't even know where he is." With the organizers sidelined, the government is now trying to buy off the rest of the protesters. Local press reports say workers at Ferro Alloy have received half their back wages and will soon get unemployment benefits or pensions. But workers say this is a fraction of what is owed—and they aren't counting on more.

> *With tensions rising, Beijing is resorting to heavy-handed tactics.*

It wasn't supposed to be this way. In 1986, Beijing announced it would start subsidizing pension payments to state-enterprise employees, and later to all urban workers. Provincial and city governments were also to contribute. The result: a mishmash of programs that mostly didn't work. Beijing tried again last year, selecting the Rust Belt province of Liaoning for a three-year pilot program. Liaoning seemed like a good bet because its governor, Bo Xilai, is widely regarded as a masterful administrator. So it was a surprise when Bo showed up at March's National People's Congress to announce that the new program wasn't working either.

It turns out there was insufficient funding from the central government, and what did arrive was probably siphoned off by local officials or managers. A solution is desperately needed. With layoffs accelerating, says Wang Dongdong, an official with the Liaoning welfare office, "time is running out."

And then there's the corruption issue. Last year, according to the National Audit Bureau, billions of dollars went missing in state enterprises as factory managers sold assets on the cheap and pocketed loans and pension proceeds. Given the allegations swirling around the closure of the Ferro Alloy factory, Beijing knows it can't stand idly by. *The Liaoyang Daily* has reported that at least 13 factory managers are being probed for corrupt activities involving more than $600,000. "If the government is clever," says Hong Kong-based labor activist Han Dongfang, "they will sacrifice some local officials."

Another solution is to use grassroots reforms to foster accountability. It's already happening in the rich coastal cities, where residents are encouraged to report graft, city officials must pass proficiency tests, and public hearings are held on everything from power price hikes to phone surcharges. So far no such democratization has been allowed in Liaoyang and other Rust Belt cities, where the enormity of the problems make such measures seem a luxury. Besides, northeastern officialdom has little patience for workers' grievances. As a result, they take them to the streets. Says labor activist Han: "The system doesn't allow the workers to have negotiations around the table. That is the sickness of the system."

Unless they spread and involve more people, the protests are unlikely to prompt real change in labor policy any time soon. And while Liaoyang workers from various factories and industries have shown unusual solidarity, there is no sign that a regional labor movement is forming—let alone a national one. For the time being, China's only sanctioned labor entity is the All-China Federation of Trade Unions, a toothless group established in 1925. "It has been extremely difficult to link up social protest in different areas," says rights activist Becquelin. "There is no independent union, because as soon as one tries to set up one, they retaliate."

That means that pressure will continue to build in China's inefficient state economy, particularly in heavy industry and agriculture. Already, a destabilizing income gap between haves and have-nots is looming. Consider that in 2000, according to the Asian Development Bank, per capita income of the top 20% of China's urban population jumped 9.6%, to $1,360. By contrast, the income of the bottom 20%—about 80 million people—grew only 2.7%, to $377 per year. "That's very worrisome," says Tang Min, the ADB's chief economist in China. Indeed it is. Until China's leaders figure out how to give their workers a peaceful way to raise their complaints, the demos will continue—and that could force real political change upon Beijing.

Growing Rich-Poor Gap, Economic Growth, Spur Crime in China[3]

By Michael Dorgan
Knight Ridder / Tribune Business News, March 27, 2002

When Lan Youming's daughter recently invited him to visit her in Beijing, just a 90-minute bus ride away, he declined. The 65-year-old retired farmer was too concerned about crime.

It wasn't the big-city crime of Beijing that frightened him, though crime of all kinds is a growing problem in the capital. It was the rising crime in Lan's seemingly serene redbrick village of 1,700 that had him worried. He feared that if he spent a night in Beijing, he might return to find his modest home stripped bare. "There are two kinds of crime," Lan said one recent afternoon as he sipped tea in the sunny main room of his courtyard home. "It is sometimes driven by destitution, and sometimes related to power." They're often linked, and his village suffers from both, he said.

Lan said corruption was mainly to blame: "Corrupt officials are taking more and more, so villages are more poor and more people are turning to crime."

Economic growth and China's growing rich-poor gap are other factors spurring crime in villages and cities throughout the country. Rising prosperity has greatly raised expectations and created new opportunities across China for gain, both legitimate and illegitimate.

Some of the more spectacular recent crimes have made headlines. For example, an ongoing investigation into a multibillion-dollar smuggling ring in the southern port city of Xiamen has snared more than 100 officials, 11 of whom have been sentenced to death.

But while big crimes cause concern, most Chinese may be more worried by the plague of lesser crimes that affect their daily lives.

China's late paramount leader Deng Xiaoping warned more than two decades ago that "flies and mosquitoes" would enter along with prosperity when China opened the window to economic reform. But few Chinese could have imagined that so many pickpockets, burglars, con men, armed robbers, pimps, prostitutes, killers and corrupt officials would climb in through the window as well.

As many as 100 million poor farmers with dreams of a better life have migrated to cities in recent years, where they often end up with the lowest paying jobs or no jobs at all. Many become prime

---

3. Article by Michael Dorgan from *Knight Ridder/Tribune Business News* March 27, 2002. Copyright © 2002 *Knight Ridder/Tribune Business News*. Reprinted with permission.

candidates for careers in crime, as do many of the unsupervised youths left behind in villages with their grandparents when their parents go off in search of work.

The full dimensions of China's crime problem are not publicly known.

Liu Renwen, a crime expert at the Chinese Academy of Social Science's Institute of Law, said studies showed that more than half of the crimes in China's cities were committed by these migrants from the countryside. He was quick to add that the criminals often are directed by urban crime bosses.

"Almost all of them come with good dreams; they don't leave the countryside with the intention to commit crime," Liu said. "But the reality is not as beautiful as their imaginations. The reality is sometimes very cruel."

Many young women who leave the countryside with promises of jobs as clerks or waitresses in cities end up as indentured sex workers in brothels or karaoke bars. Many young men, unable to find even $2-a-day jobs in construction or factories, become urban scavengers and predators, stealing everything from manhole covers to wallets.

Liu, who lives in Beijing, home to more than 3 million recent immigrants from rural areas, notes that there is a popular saying, "You're not a real Beijing resident until you've had your bicycle stolen."

The full dimensions of China's crime problem are not publicly known, because the government classifies most crime statistics as state secrets. But anecdotal evidence and the partial official statistics released suggest that few remain untouched by crime.

In a report earlier this month to the National People's Congress, China's chief prosecutor disclosed an 82 percent rise last year in crimes involving guns and bombs. And the president of the Supreme People's Court told the legislators that China's courts presided over 350 Mafia-style organized crime cases in 2001, a six-fold increase over the previous year.

Some citizens may take comfort in the performance of the nation's courts, which heard 729,958 criminal cases last year, a 31 percent increase over 2000, and claimed a 99.9 percent conviction rate.

China also tries to use heavy punishment as a deterrent, including the use of the death penalty in a wide range of crimes.

But most crimes go unpunished, experts and citizens said, partly because China's police, prosecutors and courts are often poorly trained and overloaded. Another reason is that many corrupt officials at all levels commit crimes with relative impunity.

Liu said many crimes that afflicted China's citizens were not even acknowledged as such by the government.

A theft of $50, for example, is not a crime under China's laws, even though that amount might represent half the annual income of a poor farmer. The threshold for a theft to become a crime varies by region, but typically is $60 to $100. Thefts involving lesser amounts are not prosecuted as crimes, but are treated as infractions that police can deal with as they see fit.

One problem with that arrangement, Liu said, is that police often ignore offenses that don't qualify as crimes, even though they may represent devastating losses for the victims. Another problem, villager Lan said, is that police often abuse their discretionary authority to aid corrupt local officials.

After his own village chief was caught stealing wheat two years ago, he was voted out of office but never faced any other penalties, Lan said. Even when the former chief was caught stealing corn the next year, no punishment followed.

The former chief appears to have set a standard of conduct for many in his village. Almost anything that isn't tied down and some things that are get stolen, Lan said, including farm animals, tools, even the electrical wiring for the village's irrigation system.

Violence is also becoming more common, he said, noting that members of a family whose sheep was stolen recently were stopped and beaten by the thief while they were on their way to the police station to report the theft.

Cao Wenhua, who lives in a nearby village, said crime was growing there as well.

"In Mao's time, crime was under control," said Cao, a 55-year-old janitor. "In Deng's era, it became more common. I think it comes from Deng encouraging people to get rich and telling them that being poor is despicable."

Being poor is something Cao knows.

He had hoped to have a nest egg after the government relocated his family, along with dozens of others, several years ago to make way for the expansion of a water reservoir. They were all promised settlement money, he said, but most of it was stolen by corrupt officials.

In China, Student Loans May Be Expanding Societal Gaps They Were Supposed to Close[4]

BY JIANG XUEQIN
CHRONICLE OF HIGHER EDUCATION, DECEMBER 7, 2001

Last year in August, Ma Xiaoqing arrived in Beijing, unsure how long he could stay. A month earlier, after years of diligent studying in a remote province, he had won admission to China Agricultural University, an elite university. His parents had borrowed money from neighbors to pay for Mr. Ma's first year of college—$1,000, four times his parents' annual income—and sent him on a two-day train trip to Beijing, where he had hoped to apply for a student loan to pay for the rest of his education. But after he arrived he did not know how to begin, whom to talk to, or where to go. Alone and homesick, three months later, he called his mother and said that he wanted to come home.

Mr. Ma's frustration is all too common today in China. In 1999, Chinese universities began for the first time in China's history as a socialist country to charge tuition. Before that, universities were free, and graduates were assigned jobs by the state. Beginning in the 1990s, graduates could finally choose their own futures, and the government began to cut financial support to universities, forcing them to pay more of their own way. While more opportunities for higher education were being created, students and their parents were being asked to shoulder a large financial burden. So in the same year as tuition was instituted, the Ministry of Education created a student-loan program to assist poor students.

"Not one of the newly enrolled students will be deprived of the right to study because of family financial difficulties," China's vice minister of education, Zhang Baoqing, said at the time.

Today Chinese universities charge an average of $600 annually, three-fourths of China's annual per capita income. Mr. Ma was getting a $140 discount off his university's usual tuition of $500 because he was studying zoology, a department subsidized by the government because it wants more zoologists and the field isn't a popular one. But the cost of room and board more than doubles the bill.

---

4. Article by Jiang Xueqin from *The Chronicle of Higher Educaiton* December 7, 2001. Copyright © Jian Xueqin. Reprinted with permission.

Mr. Ma's parents, like the vast majority of Chinese, are subsistence farmers, growing wheat on a small plot of land on the remote plains of Guanghan county, in Sichuan province, earning little and saving nothing. During the Mao Zedong era they suffered immense poverty; then, when Deng Xiaoping came into power in the late 1970s and freed the peasants from the communes, they saw their lives gradually improve. But in the mid-'90s, as local officials steadily increased taxes, the national government drastically cut subsidies supporting wheat prices, throwing peasants back into poverty.

> *"The student-loan program is a lie."*—Li, a laid-off worker

A Way Out

This autumn, while Mr. Ma is hunched over books in the university library, his parents will be harvesting wheat from dawn to dusk, expecting to pocket only $250 for the season, a sum that will also be their annual income. Their son's chance at a university degree is the family's only way out.

"While other parents in the village told their young kids to go find work, my mother encouraged me to go to school," Mr. Ma says.

Nowadays for poor students, going to college means getting a loan. But the ministry has conceded that not all students can obtain loans. According to its own statistics, 534,000 students have applied for what the government said would be $400-million in state education loans. Only 170,000 students received loans, and they received an average of 37 percent of what they asked for, reaching a total of $145-million. Banks refused to allocate the full $400-million for the student loans. The remaining 70 percent of the students were rejected, because the banks viewed them as poor credit risks. The free-market economy has rapidly created more places for students at state and private institutions. But it also means that those who can't pay the price will be shoved off the waiting line for enrollment.

"The student-loan program is a lie," declares Li, a laid-off worker in the southwest city of Chongqing who declined to give her full name.

After her son got a high enough score on the national entrance exam to be admitted to Chongqing Construction College, he went to the bank to apply for a student loan, but he has never heard back. The family had to borrow money from friends to pay for the first year, and is now heavily in debt and does not know where to turn. "We can only take it one step at a time," says Mrs. Zhang.

A Decentralized System

Why are stories like those of Ms. Zhang and Ma Xiaoqing proliferating? The Ministry of Education does not have the power to push universities and banks into lending to students. Like most policies in China, the national government mandate to issue student loans is carried out by local governments at their own discretion, and often, with their own money.

Regional economic disparities mean that a few local governments can pressure regional banks or local universities into offering students generous aid while the majority of places either choose to be stingy or don't have student-loan programs in place yet. These disparities are cemented by the way the ministry distributes scarce funds: The government spends less than 3 percent of the gross national product on education, and most of the money earmarked for higher education goes to a few select universities, giving a handful of them enough money to lend directly to students but leaving most universities in a position where student loans are out of the question.

Moreover, China does not yet have a system to rate people's credit.

The government spends less than 3 percent of the gross national product on education.

Unlike ordinary loans, student loans neither require collateral nor a guarantor so banks are at the mercy of each student's honesty and ability to repay the loan. "We support giving students loans but much prefer to offer them ordinary loans, which limit our risk exposure," says Cui Yiping, a Beijing bank official responsible for student loans with the Agriculture Bank of China, one of the four state banks charged with giving out student loans. Some bank officials have openly said that they will not lend to students because they believe that the odds are against new graduates finding employment.

Even when a willingness to lend exists, both universities and banks have yet to create a way to market or administer student loans, and rules vary from institution to institution. Students then are left to wander in the darkness.

"Insecure and Pessimistic"

Like Ma Xiaoqing. China Agricultural University did not have a student-loan office, counselors, or brochures. "When I first came to Beijing, I was anxious, insecure, and pessimistic," says Mr. Ma, a usually ebullient young man who talks fast and shakes his legs when seated.

"I compensated by putting all my energy into studying, and by remembering all the hard work I put into getting into university." By withdrawing into his studies, he missed the fact that there was an information meeting about student loans early in September, and that he could have applied for a loan then. Last December he called his mother.

"He told me that there was nothing he could do and that he had to come home," recalls Lai Dengyu, Mr. Ma's mother. "I told him that he couldn't give up. 'You've already made it to Beijing, and you can't quit school—schooling is too important,' I said. 'If there's nothing you can do, I'll borrow some more money.'"

Ma Xiaoqing recalls that after talking to his mother that cold December day he became depressed.

"I knew there was nothing my mother could do," he says. "I knew that our neighbors had no more money left to lend us."

Mr. Ma can count himself as one of the few lucky ones. A few days after he called his mother, a lecturer at the university told him that although he had missed the first meeting, he had one more chance. Six of his 37 classmates in the lecturer's class joined him at the loan meeting. There, a representative from the Industrial and Commercial Bank of China, another of the four state banks charged with administering student loans, explained the

---

"Chinese don't like loans, and if they don't absolutely need the money, they won't borrow it."—**Ma Xiaoqing, a student at China Agricultural University**

---

procedure for filling out the two-page application, and gave the students a short time to complete it and decide how much money they needed for the next three years.

"The meeting was not planned very well," says Mr. Ma. "No one explained to us what happens if we graduate and fail to find a job. How about if we want to go to graduate school? What happens if I study abroad? And we can only fill out the application once—we cannot apply for additional loans if the first is not enough."

"The bank representative told us that if we applied to go to graduate school we can apply for another loan," says Yang Li, one of Mr. Ma's classmates who attended an earlier meeting. "But someone had to ask before the bank representative told us this. If you don't ask, they won't tell you."

The most important question that Mr. Ma had to answer in his application form was how much money he wanted for his monthly allowance. The limit was the equivalent of $30, and Mr. Ma chose $12, just enough for food.

"Chinese don't like loans, and if they don't absolutely need the money, they won't borrow it," says Mr. Ma.

At the end of the afternoon he had to sign a contract, promising to pay back the principal and interest by 2006, three years after his graduation. He was told that the government will pay for half of the 10-percent annual interest rate. In hindsight he thinks that the process was too quick and confusing.

"It should have been more clear and transparent," he says. "I don't know much about what the loan demands and how it works, and no one bothered telling my parents, so they know nothing." Although Mr. Ma's parents are not legally responsible for repaying the loan, his future earnings will have to pay off both his own debts and theirs.

A Chaotic Start

Zhou Xiaohong, a professor of education at China's Northeast Normal University, explains that Mr. Ma's experience is a common one. Last year when the program started things were very chaotic, and students didn't know how to deal with the complex student-loan process.

"The universities did not benefit from the student-loan program so they did little to help the students," Mr. Zhou says. Wang Yan, China Agricultural University's dean of student affairs and the person responsible for student loans, believes that the current system is fine.

"We've done enough in promoting the student-loan program," she says. "Along with ICBC, we organized a lecture early in September describing the student-loan process. But since last year was our first year perhaps there were some problems. This year we've greatly improved the system, though." For example, she says, students who need a loan can arrive on campus and get one before they pay the first year's tuition.

On January 1, 2001, Mr. Ma received a notice from the bank saying that he had been awarded $1,644, enough to cover his three remaining years. Every month he goes to the bank's automatic teller machine to get his allowance, and the bank automatically wires his tuition to the university.

After his graduation, Mr. Ma will be expected to pay $150 every three months, a sum he expects he can manage. Last summer, thanks to his university's work-study program, he stayed in Beijing, working three hours a day at the university's swimming pool and pocketing $60 a month.

Many students have come to feel that, far from evening out social inequality, the student-loan program is just reinforcing it, with students who can get to the wealthier provinces prospering, and others left behind. In a pilot program, the World Bank has established a $100,000 fund at Lanzhou University, which generally is not considered to be one of the politically favored institutions, to see if it can create a better student-loan program.

But two decades of capitalism in China has led many to accept inequality.

"It's true that in other provinces students don't have access to money," says Wang Yan, the dean. "Beijing has a lot of money so it's easy for students here to borrow money. But what do you expect? Beijing is the capital, after all."

The Sickness Trap[5]

By Susan V. Lawrence
Far Eastern Economic Review, June 13, 2002

The fastest road to poverty in China today is a visit to the doctor—especially in the countryside. Ask Yang Zhengshan, a 65-year-old wheat farmer with a wispy beard and a lattice of broken veins across his weathered cheeks, who lives in the Ningxia Hui Autonomous Region in the remote northwest. Lying in bed last year, he suddenly found he couldn't sit up. "Half my body was paralyzed. I couldn't move at all," he says, fingering a straw hat he wears to protect himself from the sun.

On a village doctor's advice, he was rushed from Huoxing village to a hospital in the region's capital Yinchuan, an hour away by truck. Over the next three weeks there, doctors took four X-rays and a magnetic resonance image, or MRI, and diagnosed him as having had a stroke. They prescribed a raft of medicines, and administered injections and massages.

Yang recovered. But his bills came to $1,350, a fortune in this part of China, where people in rural areas earn an average of just $220 a year. The hospital required a hefty cash deposit when Yang checked in, and payment of his outstanding charges every three to five days. And the money all came out of his pocket because, like 90% of the 900 million people in China who live in the countryside, Yang has no medical insurance.

What saved him from ruin was having a lot of sons, he says. All four scraped together the money for the hospital. "One paid 2,000 renminbi ($240). Another paid 3,000. My sons are good children," says Yang. But his sons' savings were completely wiped out, and follow-up medications still cost him $30 a month.

It could have been a lot worse. For every tale of a family scraping by, Yang's neighbours cite a case of medical costs pushing families into poverty.

In the village next to Yang's, neighbours talk of Ma Yuqiang and his wife who last year ran up medical bills of $850—$370 for his kidney stones and $480 for her hysterectomy. They had to borrow money from relatives and friends to pay the bills. In a place where families are expected to spend hundreds of dollars on weddings for their sons despite their modest means, the Ma family had no money to bring a wife for their son into their family. Instead, in exchange for the woman's family helping to pay their debts, their son married into her family and took his earnings with him. Without his income, neighbours agree, the Mas have little chance of enjoying a comfortable old age.

With health-insurance coverage shrinking while medical costs rise far faster than incomes, China faces a humanitarian disaster that threatens to undo one of the country's proudest achievements of the last 20 years: the lifting of an estimated 210 million people out of absolute poverty. Harvard University health economist William Hsiao says his research with Chinese colleagues in several hundred Chinese counties shows that for every 10 Chinese pulled out of poverty 12 fall into poverty because of the burden of medical expenses. Health officials and outside experts now routinely identify high medical costs combined with an absence of insurance as rural China's No. 1 "poverty generator."

The danger is most acute for China's farmers, because they have lower incomes than their city brethren and almost no insurance coverage. Ministry of Health figures show that by 1999, only one in 10 people in rural areas had any health insurance—25% down

---

Health officials and outside experts now routinely identify high medical costs combined with an absence of insurance as rural China's No. 1 "poverty generator."

---

from the number four years before. Even in the cities, only 42% of residents had any insurance in 1999, a 22% drop from four years earlier. Yet in the 1990s, according to Ministry of Health statistics, the cost of an average hospital admission leapt 511% while the average cost of a visit to the doctor soared 625%—rates two to three times that of income growth.

It wasn't always this way. From the 1950s to the 1970s, under Mao Zedong, China's rural health infrastructure won accolades from the rest of the world. Mao set up village health stations, township health centres and county hospitals. At the village level, agricultural collectives paid the salaries of so-called "barefoot doctors" and put money into collective welfare funds for drugs and treatment. Patients paid modest premiums and a nominal fee for consultations and medicines. Local governments also contributed.

The system wasn't perfect. Rao Keqin, who directs the Ministry of Health's Centre for Health Statistics and Information, notes that a lack of transparency in commune accounts meant health funds were often misused, and relatives of local leaders often got better treatment than ordinary farmers. Because barefoot doctors had limited training, they only provided basic medical care. But they did administer vaccinations, prescribe simple drugs and give injections of antibiotics when needed. "It was low-cost medicine," says Rao. "Everyone could afford it. It met people's needs, because people's needs then were modest." Infant-mortality rates dropped and life expectancy soared.

After 1979, however, Deng Xiaoping dismantled the agricultural collectives in the name of reform. Because he did not make any new provisions for funding rural health care, the health infrastructure collapsed. A paper Rao co-authored last year with a Harvard School of Public Health professor, Liu Yuanli, shows that within six years of Deng taking power, rural residents covered by the Rural Cooperative Medical Systems of the Mao era fell from 90% to just 9.6%.

Barefoot doctors were left to support themselves with what they could earn from prescriptions and services such as injections and intravenous drips. In turn, farmers had to shoulder the cost of every doctor's visit and hospital admission.

Late last year, Liu and Rao's paper, written as part of a study funded by the Asian Development Bank and China's State Development and Planning Commission, found its way to the desk of China's top leader, Jiang Zemin. International experts credit its alarming statistics and uncompromising conclusions for shocking Jiang into taking an active, if belated, interest in the crisis, just months before he is due to step down as head of the Communist Party. As a result of two telephone calls this year from Jiang to China's Minister of Health, Zhang Wenkang, building a rural health-insurance system has become one of the ministry's top three priorities. "He said our emphasis must be on the countryside," Rao says Jiang told the minister. "He said we must do more here."

Yet Jiang's words serve to highlight the degree to which China's leadership has so far avoided confronting how health-care expenses are bankrupting the rural population. A 1996 national conference

---

Less Funds for the Poor

Under China's government health-care system the burden of paying for medical care is heaviest on the people who can least afford it. The World Health Organizaiton reflected that in its 2000 rankings, listing China 188th out of 191 countries in fairness of financial contributions to health care.

According to Harvard University health economist William Hsiao, a staggering 68% of Chinese government funding for medical care goes toward looking after the wealthiest 20% of the population. In the Ningxia Hui Autonomous Region, a poor area in China's northwest, 84% of the $24 million annual health-care budget goes to the 30% of the population living in urban areas.

In a paper last year, Liu Yuanli, a Harvard School of Public Health professor, and Ministry of Health official Rao Keqin point out that the central government has been cutting its share of China's health-care spending, slashing it by nearly 60% since 1980. In the rest of the world, they write: "As countries develop and their economies grow, governments assume a larger share of health spending, thus resulting in lower out-of-pocket health expenditures." In China, the opposite is true.

Susan V. Lawrence

on health care briefly took up the issue, calling for the establishment of a voluntary, community-based health safety net in the countryside. But no central government ministry was ever tasked with considering how to go about building such a system. When the Ministry of Labour and Social Security began building a safety net for the cities in late 1998, to facilitate state-owned enterprise reform, the Ministry of Health argued that the Ministry of Labour should be in charge of doing the same for the rural areas. The Ministry of Labour refused to take on the job. Only this year did China's leaders finally assign the mission to the Ministry of Health.

Jiang recently named a point man for the rural health safety net: Li Jiange, a deputy director of the State Council's Economic Restructuring Office. A national conference on the subject is tentatively scheduled for later in the year. But no one is under any illusion about the crisis easing any time soon. The biggest question is where the money for a rural insurance scheme might come from. The central government is reluctant to come up with the cash. Provincial governments say their own budgets are already stretched much too thin. Many rural residents are wary about contributing to a rural health-insurance programme because of mistrust of local officials, who often have a history of mismanaging finances. And local officials point out they are under orders to cut the number of fees levied on farmers, not increase them. A new rural tax intended to replace the fees does not include any component for health care.

China is, moreover, on the cusp of a major political transition, with not just Jiang but half the Communist Party Central Committee expected to leave office this year. If a rural health initiative is too closely associated with Jiang, experts warn, there's a danger it could be swept to one side by the new leadership.

Profits Have Priority over Care

Meanwhile medical costs keep climbing. Part of the reason, Rao says, is the different medical care patients now seek. Because of longer life expectancy, "instead of dealing with epidemics, doctors now are increasingly treating diabetes and tumours," Rao says. But as important a part of the equation is the profit motive in medical institutions from the village to the biggest cities. Harvard's Hsiao says that in many places "village doctors have basically become drug pedlars, selling the most expensive drugs and the most profitable ones" because they have to finance themselves. They also make money from intravenous drips, Hsiao says, "which they don't know how to give."

At higher levels, doctors not only prescribe unnecessary drugs, but also routinely order unnecessary tests. Yang's care is a case in point. In the West, his weakness on one side of his body would have been enough on its own to diagnose a stroke. If a doctor chose a test, it would usually be a CT scan, rather than an even more expensive MRI. Yang also would probably have been hospitalized for just two days, and then moved to a nursing home for rehabilitation and therapy. And instead of $30 a month in follow-up drugs, he would be taking cheap aspirin.

In Ningxia, Dou Wenmin, deputy director of the regions Health Bureau, says that in the absence of funding for rural health insurance, he and his colleagues do what they can to keep profitseeking doctors in the countryside in check. In six Ningxia counties that are part of a United Nations Childrens Fund project, the Health Bureau has banned village doctors from giving intravenous therapy. They've also required doctors to cut back the drugs on their shelves to 80, and to forego expensive antibiotics in favour of cheaper ones. Doctors get $7 a month each to make up for the income lost by the changes, enough to satisfy them in the four poorest counties, officials say, but not for doctors in the two better-off counties.

The Health Bureau is also trying to crack down on doctors who knowingly prescribe drugs—often fakes—produced by unlicensed manufacturers, which they buy cheaply and sell to patients at full price. Ding Zhanming, a former barefoot doctor with a clinic in Huoxing, says inspectors drop by unannounced several times a month to match official receipts to his stocks of 150 kinds of drugs. To prevent doctors reusing single-use needles, used needles should be turned in and checked off against the number bought.

On a busy afternoon, all but one patient who comes into Ding's clinic emerges with a stack of medicines. Usually, a patient receives an injection of antibiotics, too, for ailments as diverse as impetigo and toothache, though the effectiveness of a single dose, or even two doses a day apart, is unclear. But Ding has a strong reputation. No one admits to begrudging him his bills of $1–2 per visit.

"People come here with small illnesses, and they don't spend much money," Ding explains. "Most people here fear the big illnesses. The ones they have to go to hospital for. It usually costs them at least 5,000 renminbi, in cash. They need relatives and friends to lend them money. This is what people fear most."

From China, with Love[6]

By Christen Pears
Northern Echo, February 18, 2002

Sitting on the floor, watching a Sooty video together, Suzanna and Catherine Wallis seem like any other pair of sisters. But the six-year-old girls couldn't have had a more different start to life.

Suzanna was born in China and abandoned by her parents. She spent the first four years of her life in an orphanage and, for most of the time, was strapped into a wooden chair. Physically, she was like an 18-month-old baby and couldn't walk or talk.

Around 30 million babies are born in China every year. Up to one million of them, mainly girls and the disabled, are abandoned by their parents and many of them die from exposure. Others are picked up by street gangs and used for professional begging. The lucky ones are taken to state-run orphanages but even there, their chances of survival are slim. A chronic lack of funding and expertise means that some institutions have death rates of 80 per cent or even higher.

In the 1990s, the world became aware of the plight of China's orphans through the television documentary, *The Dying Rooms*. It was around this time that the charity Childhood Friends was set up by Beverley Wallis. It's not a large organisation but it has launched a number of successful fostering programmes and funded new equipment and additional orphanage staff.

Beverley knew what conditions were like in the orphanages and when her daughter Catherine was less than a year old, she decided to adopt a child from China.

"The main reason I decided to do it was that I didn't want Catherine to be an only child," she explains. "I was single at the time. I didn't necessarily see myself having another baby but I had a good income and a nice home. I know there are children who need adoption in this country but adopting in China seemed like the right thing to do."

She initially planned to adopt a baby but one of her colleagues had met Suzanna through her work and suggested she try to adopt her.

In some countries, like Romania, adopters are allowed to approach families directly, but in China, everything is regulated by the state. Beijing sets a yearly quota for each orphanage of the number of children who can be put up for adoption and, perhaps understandably, the staff choose the ones they think are most likely to find new homes. This means children with disabilities rarely have the chance to be adopted. Suzanna, who had a cleft palette, was one of those children.

"It's fairly unusual to choose a child to adopt but she probably wouldn't have been adopted otherwise. The orphanage director was very pleased, although he thought I was crazy because there were plenty of healthy babies I could adopt."

Beverley had seen photographs of Suzanna but the first time she met her daughter was when she went to pick her up from the orphanage.

"It must have been strange experience for her but she never cried, she never complained. When we came back to this country, she settled in brilliantly. She grew very quickly and within about eight months she'd just about caught up."

The family now live in Corbridge in Northumberland. Suzanna turned six last week and the windowsill in the living room is cov-

---

"One woman, who's one of our foster parents, works as a cleaner and she's found 100 children dumped in bins over the last few years."—**Beverly Wallis of Childhood Friends**

---

ered with birthday cards. She goes to the local school, where she is coping well, and has lots of friends.

"She does everything Catherine does and she isn't treated any differently. Some parents send their children to learn Mandarin and teach them all about China but that just makes them different. I'm sure when Suzanna's older she'll be interested in China and I'll be happy for her to learn Mandarin or take her to China. But I think at a young age, you have to treat them as one of your own children, not something you've just borrowed from another culture."

Suzanna is a happy, lively little girl and although she clearly remembers being in the orphanage, she doesn't seem to be affected by it. When I ask her about her life in China, she says without hesitation: "It was very cold and I was just sitting in a seat all the time. I didn't like it very much."

She then disappears upstairs with Catherine and, a few minutes later, they come back, carrying a pile of photograph albums. Suzanna sidles up to me on the sofa and shows me some of the pictures.

"That's me in the orphanage," she says, as she points at the album. The photo shows a small, pale girl with cropped hair and a large scar on her upper lip from surgery. She's almost unrecognisable.

There are other photographs in the albums taken by Beverley during her visits to China. From the outside, the orphanages look impressive, some with gleaming white walls and towers that look like something from Disneyworld. Inside, it's a different story. Row upon row of cots are crammed into small rooms. Disabled children stare despondently at the camera while in others, thin, sickly-looking babies lie helplessly on their mattresses, some of them clearly dying.

"It's an enormous problem," says Beverley. "One woman, who's one of our foster parents, works as a cleaner and she's found 100 children dumped in bins over the last few years. The orphanages just don't have the money or the expertise to look after these children and sadly, a lot of them do die."

And for the ones who survive, the future is bleak unless they are lucky enough to be adopted. Most of them will stay in the orphanage until they are old enough to employed, usually in menial, low-paid work.

"Some of them just disappear and they probably go the factories as slave labour," explains Beverley. She would like to see more people adopt but believes many of them are put off by negative publicity and the lengthy and complicated adoption process.

"One of the major problems in this country is that people are always being told that the children come with problems, they're institutionalised. Of course there's going to be an element of truth in that but what they forget is that children are individuals and different children are going to respond in different ways. There's nothing to say that if you have your own child, there aren't going to be problems."

Prospective parents are assessed by social services in the same way they would be if they were adopting a child from this country and the costs can be prohibitive. In China, this can be as much as (GBP) 3,000.

There are, however, organisations, such as OASIS, which can guide prospective parents through process.

"Virtually everyone who adopts from abroad is a member of OASIS. They provide all the information and support you need and can put you in touch with people who have already been through it. A lot of people find it invaluable because, without that, they probably wouldn't even know where to start."

Many Unhappy with Chinese Rule[7]

BY KARL SCHOENBERGER
MERCURY NEWS, JULY 1, 2002

The sidewalks are still jammed with the vibrant bustle of shoppers, businessmen and tourists, and the ferry ride across the harbor still affords a glorious view of a skyline studded with modernistic towers. But today, exactly five years after China took vague stewardship over Hong Kong, the former British colony is a deeply troubled place.

Beijing's leaders had pledged to preserve Hong Kong's traditions of free-market capitalism and civil liberties under the banner of "one country, two systems," but those guarantees continue to be eroded, government critics say.

"I don't like way things are going," growled a taxi driver named Wong, as he wheeled in front of the Star Ferry terminal, a corroding relic of colonial times. "The government hasn't taken care of the little people in Hong Kong. They just care about their friends in China." Beyond local democracy and economic prosperity, what's at stake in this experiment in governance is the prospect of Taiwan's peaceful reunification with the mainland—an issue that remains one of East Asia's most menacing security flash points. Hong Kong is widely seen as a model for what might happen to Taiwan should it rejoin the Chinese mainland.

Hong Kong officials attribute public unhappiness with the administration of Chief Executive Tung Chee Hwa to economic forces that are out of his control. After recovering from the 1997–98 regional financial crisis, Hong Kong markets took another nose dive when the speculative dot-com bubble burst in the United States. Unemployment has more than doubled in five years, to a record 7.4 percent, and a deflationary spiral is setting in.

On top of all that, Hong Kong has lost its role as a middleman for the China trade, especially since China joined the World Trade Organization last year and no longer needs a broker to deal with the West.

Against this backdrop, Tung, the avuncular Hong Kong shipping tycoon anointed by Beijing to run the territory in 1997, begins his second five-year term today under a cloud of doubt over his ability to redefine Hong Kong's role in the global economy and protect its political autonomy.

"Expectations have been raised and dashed repeatedly over the past five years, and cynicism has set in," said Michael DeGolyer, a political science professor who directs research at the Transition Project at Hong Kong Baptist University.

Economic Troubles

Tung, who ran unopposed for his second term before an appointed electoral committee, is struggling with accusations that his administration is drifting and lacks accountability. He is floundering in his efforts to revitalize the sagging economy, resorting to government promotion of high technology schemes that many analysts say don't suit Hong Kong's quick-return entrepreneurial culture.

> *In general, . . . optimism about the future of Hong Kong has plummeted, from 60 percent in June 1997 to 26 percent today.*

Tung's critics describe him as a politically inept and indecisive leader who is more interested in pleasing his mainland masters than listening to the concerns of Hong Kong's nearly 7 million people. The public is disenchanted: Tung's job approval crashed from 50 percent when he first took office five years ago to 33 percent in April, according to surveys by the Transition Project. Of the 751 respondents, 61 percent said they did not want him to be re-elected.

In general, the survey also found that optimism about the future of Hong Kong has plummeted, from 60 percent in June 1997 to 26 percent today.

To restore confidence, Tung inaugurated a new layer of government this month, installing a quasi-Cabinet that purportedly will widen responsibility for policy decision-making and respond more effectively to diverse interests in the community.

"Our goal is not to lose public support," said Stephen Lam, the chief executive's spokesman, explaining the need for the restructuring. But at the same time, Lam also articulated an "emperor's new clothing" attitude that critics say typifies Tung's office: "The political worries that people had about the future in 1997 have been swept away."

That view doesn't square with Hong Kong's pro-democracy advocates, who point to a lack of transparency in Tung's government that has dampened public confidence.

For example, early in his first term when Hong Kong's frothy real estate market was collapsing, Tung abruptly canceled an ambitious public housing program, without legislative debate and without consulting with officials in his own administration responsible for the program. Tung had pledged before he took office in 1997 to address the critical lack of affordable housing.

More recently, Tung's administration demonstrated a penchant for secrecy when officials refused to grant a visa, without explanation, to activist Harry Wu. The former Milpitas resident, who had served 19 years in a Chinese prison for advocating human rights, is a naturalized U.S. citizen, and was scheduled to make a public appearance last Tuesday in Hong Kong. In April, Wu was deported after arriving at the airport in Hong Kong and denied the entry visa that ordinarily is extended automatically to Americans.

Lam, the government spokesman, said immigration officials did not need to explain their actions in these cases.

That's a distinct change from five years ago, critics say.

"Five years ago, we didn't have any dissidents in Hong Kong. It was normal to criticize the government," bemoaned Margaret Ng, an outspoken human rights lawyer who holds a seat in the Legislative Council. She complains it is increasingly difficult to get police permission to stage peaceful street demonstrations in Hong Kong. "People like me are being sidelined, put out in the cold."

Immigration Fight

Perhaps the single most worrisome event in Tung's first term was Chinese intervention that trumped a court decision on the right of abode in Hong Kong for the relatives of local residents who were left behind in the mainland. Fearing social calamity from a massive influx of Chinese crossing the border, Hong Kong authorities have cracked down aggressively on illicit immigration and enforce a strict quota of 150 legal newcomers a day.

But the government lost a test case on the right of abode before the Court of Final Appeal in 2000. Tung sought remedy from China's National People's Congress, which did not nullify the ruling but passed legislation interpreting the Basic Law in a way that prevented the Hong Kong court's decision from setting a precedent for future litigation. Civil libertarians cried foul, accusing Tung of inviting unwarranted Chinese intrusion into Hong Kong's supposedly independent legal system.

"I get really angry about this criticism, because it comes from the legal elite in Hong Kong and they are lying," said Shiu Sin Por, director of One Country Two Systems Research Institute, a pro-government think tank. Shiu became visibly agitated and red in the face when the topic was raised. "They know this case is not undermining the rule of law in Hong Kong, but they use it for political purposes."

Two Big Projects

To save his legacy and re-energize this special administrative region, as Hong Kong is known, Tung is placing his bets on two grand projects.

The first is Hong Kong Cyberport, a controversial residential and hotel project where a politically wired developer, local telecom operator Richard Li, acquired the right to use government-owned land without open competitive bidding.

The other big project is the Hong Kong Science and Technology Park, inspired by a similar high-tech industrial park in Taiwan, but coming on line some 20 years later.

A beaming Tung officiated at the park's opening ceremony on Thursday, delivering a pep talk on how high-tech investment and local research and development will marry with existing service industries to make Hong Kong more competitive in the global economy.

Chiu Hsiang Chung, chief editor of the respected *Hong Kong Economic Journal*, is skeptical about Tung's sanguine vision. The technology industry, which requires long-term planning and delayed profits, is not a good match for Hong Kong's business culture.

"You cannot create a Silicon Valley by government order," Chiu said. "It takes a special culture for that to happen, and we don't have it."

III. Human Rights

Editor's Introduction

The issue of human rights has frequently strained China's relations with many nations. Policymakers, journalists, political activists, and religious leaders throughout the world who cherish democracy, the due process of law, and the freedom of expression and religion have been outraged by reports of human rights abuses by the Chinese government, including the persecution of religious groups and political dissidents. This section looks at several examples of the human rights abuses of which China has been accused and considers how the Chinese government has responded to those accusations.

In the first article, Jonathan Manthorpe recalls the brutality of the Cultural Revolution, which caused great upheaval in China from 1966–76 and resulted in the deaths of millions of people. In 1966 Mao Tse-tung successfully mobilized millions of young people in the Red Guards in a movement to preserve the ideals of China's proletarian revolution. The Red Guards swept through China, terrorizing much of the population and targeting those who Mao branded enemies of the revolution. "No one was safe," Manthorpe writes. "Friends and relatives denounced each other. Human decency was discarded as counter-revolutionary treason."

The Cultural Revolution may have ended, but various forms of intolerance remain in China, particularly with regard to religious observance. Although China is officially atheist, it does allow limited religious worship to those groups which have registered with the state and are closely monitored by the authorities. Religious groups that defy the government often experience persecution. In her article from *China Brief*, Nina Shea, a leading human rights activist, writes that many Chinese Christians are forced to worship in underground churches because their denominations are not approved by the state. China's leaders view the growth of religion as a threat to their authority and have intensified the persecution of Christians during the 1990s. Shea writes that Chinese acts of repression against Christians include arrest, beatings, torture, and imprisonment in labor camps for "re-education."

In the next article, John Gittings documents China's well-publicized campaign against the Dalai Lama, the exiled political and spiritual leader of Tibet. The Dalai Lama was forced to flee Tibet in 1959 after the Chinese Communists brutally put down a rebellion by his supporters and fellow Buddhists. Since then, the Dalai Lama has become a symbol of resistance to Chinese oppression and has earned the respect and admiration of many people around the world. Although China has attempted to suppress Buddhism in Tibet by imprisoning and killing thousands of monks and nuns and destroying Buddhists monasteries over the years, Gittings observes that the Dalai Lama still enjoys the support of many Tibetans.

During the last few years, the Chinese authorities have been particularly preoccupied with another religious group, a spiritual cult known as Falun Gong. In the Tokyo *Daily Yomiuri*, Juliet Rowan traces the origins of Falun Gong to the teachings of Li Hongzhi, who combined elements of Buddhism and Taoism with Qigong exercises to produce a hybrid system of beliefs and practices. Falun Gong has attracted millions of followers who have sought to explore their spirituality, but its growing popularity prompted Li to flee China in 1998 because he feared for his life. After approximately 10,000 Falun Gong practitioners held a protest in Beijing in April 1999, China immediately outlawed the cult and began persecuting it. "Reports of torture and abuse against practitioners in the camps and prisons have been widespread," Rowan writes, "sparking condemnation from world leaders and human rights groups like Amnesty International."

As Qinglian He writes in *Academe*, the publication of the American Association of University Professors, the Chinese government also restricts academic freedom. Scholars, teachers, and intellectuals are prohibited from studying Western democracies and discouraged from conducting research into the Cultural Revolution. When studying government "reform" policies, scholars are expected to reach positive conclusions. According to He, scholars who dissent from the official line are punished with the loss of their jobs and the censorship of their books and articles.

In this section's final article, by Jasper Becker for the *South China Morning Post*, the writer discusses Hong Kong's decision to expel the political dissident Harry Wu in April 2002 when Wu visited Hong Kong in order to attend a literature festival. Though Hong Kong served for decades as a sanctuary for politicians and writers who ran afoul of the Communist Party, Becker warns that continued censorship and repression may cause Hong Kong to "lose its unique importance in the Chinese world" as a beacon of freedom to the mainland. Becker also argues that contemporary Chinese literature suffers from both censorship and commercialism.

Why Did a Nation Go Mad?[1]

By Jonathan Manthorpe
Vancouver Sun, March 23, 2002

It is one of those little ironies without which life would be a much less jovial affair that when China began to embrace the market economy in the 1980s, items that immediately flew off store shelves were momentoes of The Great Proletarian Cultural Revolution.

It was, of course, foreigners who rushed to buy copies of the *Little Red Book* of the thoughts of Chairman Mao Tse-tung, watches with his portrait on the dial face and reproductions of the posters that glorified the purity of the socialist spirit of the gangs of Red Guards who wreaked havoc, death and destruction for a decade from 1966.

That is understandable. What little the first outsiders in any numbers to visit China in the 1980s knew of this previously closed society was from footage of events like carefully choreographed rallies of hundreds of thousands of Red Guards in Tiananmen Square. More than that, there had been a vogue among young people in the West for Mao and the apparent ideological certainties his idolatry allowed. This cult was aided by almost universal ignorance about what was actually happening in China, but was fuelled by youthful, sentimental idealism, especially in the uncertain times of the Vietnam War.

It was the same people a decade later who so eagerly gobbled up the roughly-hewn copies of Cultural Revolution memorabilia and other Mao bric-a-brac at the Friendship Store on Beijing's Jianguomenwai.

Since then, the art of the Cultural Revolution has developed a cult following, primarily in the West. There are now whole street markets and even reputable art dealers in Beijing whose main business is the art work of that period of chaos.

And with that fixation has come not only a demand for genuine relics of this strange period when the world's most populous nation went mad, but an academic sub-culture that, in its enthusiasm to dissect the art of the revolution, has pressed right up to the boundaries of reason.

---

1. Article by Jonathan Manthorpe from *Vancouver Sun* March 23, 2002. Copyright © 2002 *Vancouver Sun*. Reprinted with permission.

Those two strands have come together in Vancouver this weekend with a two-day international conference at the Emily Carr Institute of Art & Design on Granville Island and an exhibition at the Belkin Gallery at the University of British Columbia that runs until May 26.

> *What happened is easy to recount. Why it happened as it did remains unresolved.*

Among Chinese now in early middle age who lived through the Cultural Revolution it was a seminal experience. But for their children it seems to be largely irrelevant.

Before writing this article, I contacted several young Chinese friends in their early 20s who have seen the exhibition. One said: "To be honest, I can't understand it and can't feel it."

But I have many friends of her mother and father's generation for whom the Cultural Revolution remains an abiding nightmare and one for which they still cannot find a satisfactory explanation.

The Chinese Communist Party, whose institutional base and legitimacy in power were cracked and shaken by the Cultural Revolution, still does not encourage examination of that period. But there is no doubt to have been a target of the Red Guards 30 years ago is a very helpful political credential in modern China.

Many of the generation of party officials, now in their mid to late 50s, currently assuming power in Beijing wear the scars of that period with discreet pride.

Yet how was it that a country with perhaps the world's most elaborate cultural bonds and social mores became so bestial?

What happened is easy to recount. Why it happened as it did remains unresolved.

The most common judgment is that after the cataclysmic failure of his development policies in the 1950s, the Great Leap Forward, Mao felt his power slipping away. He launched the Cultural Revolution to remove all opposition to himself in the Communist Party and to maintain his supremacy.

Others think Mao was genuinely outraged to see his proletarian revolution being undermined by the ascendancy of the intellectual, managerial and technical classes in the wake of the failure of the Great Leap.

Mao believed the purpose of the communist revolution of the 1940s was to change human nature and to create finer beings. But, to quote a leading China analyst and author Graham Hutchings, everywhere Mao looked he saw "the bourgeoisie were staging a comeback. Communist leaders, including his closest comrades, were 'revisionists' and 'capitalists.'"

Those feelings were shared, though not in quite those terms, by many ordinary people for whom the Great Leap Forward had been a personal disaster. They saw in the Communist Party leadership a new imperial elite; distant and authoritarian.

But in Mao, to quote Hutchings again, they found "a messianic leader, one far above the fray of bureaucratic politics, a great teacher—both of the Chinese and of oppressed peoples everywhere."

Mao's strategy went far beyond a simple internal party putsch. First he made sure of the allegiance of the army chief Lin Biao, then he threw everyone of authority, status or stature to the mob.

Red Guards, often under army direction, launched a reign of terror against everyone from school teachers to the very top echelons of the Communist Party. No one was safe. Every action was suspect. Even politically incorrect thoughts could be a death sentence. Friends and relatives denounced each other. Human decency was discarded as counter-revolutionary treason.

Liu Shaoqi, once Mao's designated successor, was declared "a traitor, renegade and scab." He died in prison in 1969.

Party secretary Deng Xiaoping, the man who would eventually pick up the pieces of a shattered China after Mao's death in 1976 and launch the country on the road to economic reform, was banished to a farm where he looked after pigs, repaired tractors and bided his time.

It is still impossible to put reliable numbers on the suffering. The party has admitted that 100 million people were "treated unjustly." The death toll was probably in the hundreds of thousands and perhaps millions.

Some parts of China fell into virtual civil war, with rival factions battling for power with heavy artillery. There is also credible documentation that after some of these battles the victors ate the flesh of the vanquished to crown their supremacy.

As well as the human cost, a significant portion of China's cultural heritage was destroyed in the name of discarding outdated values. Libraries were burned, ancient temples disfigured or demolished, scrolls and paintings trampled in the mud.

In the end the Cultural Revolution died of exhaustion and with the death of Mao in September 1976. Mao's venomous widow, Jiang Qing, tried to revive and prolong it by seizing power with her Gang of Four.

But she was no match for Deng Xiaoping, by then rehabilitated from the pig farm. Jiang and her gang were arrested only days after Mao's death and their trial was in reality an indictment of the dead Chairman.

Jiang committed suicide in prison in 1991.

China's Crackdown on Christians[2]

By Nina Shea
China Brief, January 17, 2002

"These few days, all of those arrested have been badly beaten by the police. Ma and her boy Longfeng were both beaten almost to death. Li Enhui fell unconscious and was awakened with cold water and beaten again. They did this to her non-stop for seven days and seven nights. Xiao Yajun was also questioned seven days and seven nights. On July 20, we heard the news that Yu, who was arrested in Ma's house, had been tortured to death."

This horrifying account of China's renewed determination to eradicate independent Christian churches was described in a letter, dated December 31, 2001, from members of an underground Christian church in China, which was then smuggled to the West. It reveals graphic details and new information about the Chinese government's crackdown on Pastor Gong Shengliang and his South China Church in China's central Hubei province.

Pastor Gong had been sentenced to death on December 5 on charges of operating an "evil cult" and on apparently trumped-up charges of rape and assault. The month-long period for deciding his appeal was extended on January 5 by a Hubei court following sharp international protest.

The letter, written by two underground Christian women reports that, in efforts to find and apprehend Pastor Gong and suppress the South China Church, police arrested sixty-three congregants, severely beating at least twenty-five Christians and torturing some with electric prods. The person whom the authors write was tortured to death is Yu Zhongju, a young mother from Zhongxiang, who had been arrested last May in a private house connected with Pastor Gong's congregation. She died in police custody in late July, after having being beaten. According to her family, police informed them of Yu's death on July 20, after her body had begun to decompose. The police paid the family, warning them not to raise the matter further. There has been no official investigation of the case.

Gu Xuegui, a Christian man connected with Pastor Gong's church is also said to have disappeared while in police custody, probably sometime in October. A congregant from Puyang City, Henan province last saw Gu in a prison vehicle with his face showing signs of beatings. His family later received information that he had died under severe torture.

---

2. Article by Nina Shea from *China Brief* January 17, 2002. Copyright © 2002 Jamestown Foundation. Reprinted with permission.

The letter relates that two women, Li Tongjin and Chi Tongyuan, from Shayang, tortured by police with electric prods, resulting in blisters and burns all over their bodies. The torture was reported to have been used to force them to testify that they had had sexual relations with Pastor Gong. One woman was later able to telephone her brother and report her situation, saying, "be ready to come to pick up my body. I may either be beaten to death or sentenced to death."

The letter reports numerous other cases from May through December 2001 of brutal police beatings of the congregants in Hubei, Henan, Hebei and Sichuan provinces. It states that Pastor Gong himself was apprehended by the police on August 8 and then kicked and beaten by government security forces.

The South China Church is known within the Chinese underground Christian community and to churches in the United States. Founded by Gong in 1991 as a break-off group from Peter Xu's All Ranges Church "Quan Fan Wei" [also known as Total Scope Church or Born Again movement], it is a large evangelical congregation estimated to have at least 50,000 members in eight provinces in China. It is respected as an orthodox Christian group

---

The Chinese authorities seem to be systematically targeting Christian churches that have not registered with the state.

---

among the underground Chinese Christians with whom I spoke. Pastor Gong is well known within Chinese Christian circles as a third-generation Christian from a pious family, married with several children. Now being held in the Jingmen detention center in his native Hubei Province, Gong had been in hiding for several months after the Public Security Bureau placed him on a most wanted list for unauthorized religious activity.

Systematic Targeting

The Chinese authorities seem to be systematically targeting Christian churches that have not registered with the state, thereby submitting to state control, and which have been deemed "evil cults" in official documents. Around the same time we received the letter, we also learned of Li Guangqiang, a Hong Kong resident with the "Shouters" another evangelical underground church in China, who was also recently issued an "evil cult" indictment, possibly carrying the death penalty, by a Fujian court, for smuggling 33,000 bibles into China.

An August 9, 2001, "top secret" government document bearing the official seal of the General Squad of National Security and Defense of Beijing Bureau of Public Security, labeled the South China Church an "evil cult." The official document orders "the security squad, surveillance squad, domestic defense squad, relics protection squad and all the local public security offices" to carry out the arrest of Gong and other top leaders of the church and the "complete demolition of [the church's] organizational system." Given the source of the document, it is inconceivable that this directive did not originate at the highest levels of the Chinese government.

To a greater or lesser extent, China has repressed religion throughout the fifty years of Communist Party rule. Its aim has been to make religion serve the interests of the communist state until it disappears from Chinese society. This remains the dominant view. State religious policy, as explained by Chinese president Jiang Zemin in March 1996 is to "actively guide religion so that it can be adapted to socialist society." Ye Xiaowen, the hardliner heading the Religious Affairs Bureau (RAB), in 1996, also urged the "handling" of religious matters according to the dictates of Lenin and declared that "we will gradually weaken the influence of religion."

In the 1950s, Mao Zedong sought to control religion through government-controlled religious groups and the total suppression of uncooperative religious leaders through brutal labor camp terms, murder or exile. In the Cultural Revolution of the 1960s and 1970s, Mao closed all places of worship and tried to extinguish religion altogether. Since Mao's death in 1976, the government has tolerated some religious expression, but only within government-registered organizations. The constitution, in Article 36, guarantees freedom of religious belief but elsewhere it sets forth sweeping exceptions and qualifications to the right and states that it only protects religious activities that are "normal," without defining the term.

The collapse of Soviet Communism and the Tiananmen Square democracy demonstrations in June 1989 shook the leaders in Beijing profoundly. In 1991, the government issued Document 6, which called for a crackdown against unregistered religious groups and reaffirmed its goal of creating a "materialistic," "scientific," and atheistic society. Repression against underground religious groups rose again in 1994 after Beijing issued Decrees 144 and 145, mandating the registration of religious groups. This was followed in the late 1990s with the "strike hard" campaign and the anticult laws, aimed at "eradicating" unregistered groups.

Rules to Abide by, or . . .

Religious leaders cannot preach outside of their own area. They and their venue must be approved by the government. Religious services and members are subject to monitoring. Sermons must stick to approved topics under penalty of arrest. Seminaries and schools for theological training exist but are tightly controlled: Students, the Chinese authorities believe, must be "politically reliable." Children are barred by law from being baptized, educated in religion or attending public worship services. Registration requires that churches desist from speaking about the Second Coming of Christ, the gifts of the Spirit, the story of Creation in Genesis, certain sections of the Catholic Catechism and the evils of abortion. The "Patriotic" Protestant churches have to be organized in the same undifferentiated church body. Many unregistered places of worship have been shut down or bulldozed in recent years. Bibles and other religious literature can only be printed with government permission, and legally obtained through government-approved sources.

Beijing controls the five "authorized" religions (Protestantism, Catholicism, Buddhism, Islam and Taoism) by the Religious Affairs Bureau (RAB), controlled by the United Front Work Department, itself controlled by the Central Committee of the Communist Party. In turn, Party officials, by law must be atheists. The RAB registers and controls all religious groups through the Three-Self Patriotic movement and the China Christian Council for Protestants, the Catholic Patriotic Association and Bishops Conference for Catholics, and similar patriotic associations for Buddhists, Muslims and Taoists.

The heightened crackdown may stem from frustration and political insecurity as authorities observe the astonishing revival of religion throughout China particularly through unsanctioned groups. Since the end of the Cultural Revolution, China's Christian churches, registered and underground, Catholic and Protestant, have been experiencing explosive growth. Thirteen million Protestants are registered with the government. Unregistered Protestants may number over 50 million, in house-churches, so named because services are held in houses.

China has more Christian prisoners and detainees than any other country in the world.

Along with the current crackdown, China's government is pushing an aggressive public relations campaign to convince the West that there is no religious persecution in China, that whatever incidents of repression occur are either the unauthorized acts of "overzealous cadres" or else necessary measures against dangerous criminals, cultists and practitioners of "abnormal" religious activities. Levelling rape charges is a favored way of morally discrediting Christian pastors.

China has more Christian prisoners and detainees than any other country in the world. Three-year's "reeducation" in labor camps is the norm for such prisoners. Like political and other prisoners, Christian prisoners are held in deplorable conditions, with many forced to work as veritable slaves in labor camps.

We were told that giving China WTO status, granting it Permanent Normal Trade Relations status, awarding it the 2008 Olympic Games would all have moderating effects on China. Instead what we are seeing are the most draconian measures against Christian leaders since the anti-cult law was adopted three years ago. China continues to arrogate to itself the rights to determine religious doctrine, determine what is Christian heterodoxy, and designate religious leaders in direct violation of the international human rights covenant that it has signed.

It is urgent that President Bush, who has on several occasions publicly deplored religious persecution in China, speak out now against these latest unspeakable assaults on religious freedom. He should reconsider his state visit to Beijing scheduled for late February. He should not be raising a toast with the Chinese president while Christian leaders languish in China's torture chambers because they refuse to submit to the control of the Communist Party.

Cultural Clash in Land on the Roof of the World[3]

By John Gittings
Guardian, February 8, 2002

It is early morning outside the Potala Palace, the former home of the Dalai Lama, pilgrims from all over Tibet have begun the sacred circuit—and the Chinese flag is flying in the breeze.

Nomads with sunburnt faces as dark as their cloaks, Khampa ex-warriors with red tassels in their hair, farmers with leggings, their wives with striped aprons, plus ordinary folk from the city, old and young, walk briskly in the grey dawn.

Many twirl their prayer wheels, some prostrate themselves on mats, and one or two even drive a sheep before them around the circuit. The lucky animal is then allowed to live to the end of its natural days.

It is an advertisement of sorts for the religious freedom that China says is fully allowed in Tibet. "How can the foreign press accuse us of suppressing religion," asks an official, "when you can see it in the streets?"

The Potala receives an average of 800 pilgrims a day. It works out at about a 10th of the entire Tibetan population every year. However, the Chinese flag flying boldly—provocatively, even—in front of the Potala is a reminder that this is freedom within limits. The vast stretch of paved space behind it has been built since I was last in Lhasa. With its flagpole and ornamental lights, it is a miniature Tiananmen Square exported to Tibet.

A Chinese official confirms for the first time unofficial reports that in August 1999 the flag was targeted by a pro-independence Tibetan activist.

"Of course the Dalai [Lama] clique is trying to obstruct the modernisation of Tibet," exclaims the region's planning director, Wang Dianyuan. "Didn't they try to blow up the flagpole two years ago?"

The "clique" is also blamed for earlier explosions at the gate of a government headquarters in Lhasa, and outside the home of a senior pro-Beijing official.

Virtually all Tibetans in the region or abroad who call for independence accept the supreme authority of the Dalai Lama who has condemned any violence. However, there is a radical minority in favour of stronger action.

Another official admits that large numbers of Tibetans still support the Dalai Lama. "That many people believe in the Dalai Lama is well known," says Tu Deng, the Tibetan head of the religious affairs committee that enforces government policy. "Our main task is to help people understand his real character." Mr. Tu describes the Dalai Lama as "a splittist and an enemy of China" whose picture is therefore banned in public places.

This has created a bizarre situation in which the Chinese admit that the Dalai Lama is still the spiritual leader of Tibetan Buddhism but have airbrushed him out of the picture.

After performing the sacred circuit, the pilgrims file through the Potala, home of successive dalai lamas since the 17th century, in the prescribed clockwise circuit. Foreigners and Chinese tourists are conducted rudely against the flow in an uneasy mix. There is a plan to segregate the two, with one group admitted in the morning and the other in the afternoon.

In front of the most holy chapel in the Potala, a nomad from the plateau hands her tiny baby wrapped in a sheepskin to an older child, and prostrates herself on the floor. A smartly dressed young

---

The Chinese admit that the Dalai Lama is still the spiritual leader of Tibetan Buddhism but have airbrushed him out of the picture.

---

lady from Lhasa lies down alongside. Both then climb a wooden ladder to touch their foreheads against the statue of Arya Lokeshvara dating from the 7th century.

A party of Chinese tourists clamber up noisily behind; one of them leans against the shrine and takes a call on his mobile.

Monasteries Destroyed

"Some monks in the monasteries tell us this is just a performance for the tourists," says another foreigner who travelled widely without an official guide. It is generally assumed that some monks are spying for the authorities.

It is not as simple as that. On the roof of the Lhasa's Jokhang temple, Tibet's most sacred site, groups of monks are disputing theology with an enthusiasm that can hardly be feigned. Two seated monks question a third who stands before them, clapping his hands in triumphant emphasis when he concludes a point.

Nowhere else in the People's Republic of China does Beijing have to cope with a population so overwhelmingly attached to a non-communist ideology, and the monasteries are the focus for this central contradiction in Chinese rule.

Tibet's religious character has survived a decade of persecution during the Cultural Revolution (1966–76) when almost every monastery was destroyed by Red Guard factions among the Chinese and a much smaller number of radical Tibetans.

I am given official figures claiming that before the 1959 rebellion when the Dalai Lama fled Tibet, there were 110,000 monks and nuns living in some 2,000 monasteries across the region. Now there are said to be 47,500 monks and nuns in 1,700 religious establishments which have been rebuilt with Chinese state funds and offerings by local communities.

The figures are unreliable. An earlier Chinese version puts the original figure of monasteries at 2,700. Exiles claim there were thousands more before the mass destruction which began after the 1959 rebellion and culminated in the Cultural Revolution (1966–68) when Chinese Red Guards and Tibetan radicals joined forces.

Religion was completely banned during the Cultural Revolution, when monks were sent to prison or to work in the fields. Prayer flags and other displays of faith were also prohibited.

The "excesses" of that period were denounced in the early 1980s when religion was allowed a reprieve but the Chinese attitude

---

"The centre [in Beijing] demands that we should maintain stability in Tibet and weaken the influence of religion."—Dan Zeng, the Tibetan Communist party leader

---

remains equivocal. Last December the official *Tibet Daily* said that it is necessary to "wipe out the negative influence of religion."

The number of monks is lower now because in the past, officials explain, under the Dalai Lama's "feudal rule," families were forced to send sons to the monasteries. There is also a ban on admitting people of 15 or under to become acolytes because they should be "receiving normal education."

Despite official tolerance for everyday worship, senior officials have described Buddhism as a long-term obstacle to the transformation of Tibet.

"The centre [in Beijing] demands that we should maintain stability in Tibet and weaken the influence of religion," said Dan Zeng, the Tibetan Communist party leader, at an education conference three years ago. He added that the Chinese president, Jiang Zemin, had endorsed the campaign launched in 1996 to conduct "patriotic education in the monasteries."

Mr. Tu claims that the campaign has been successful, although "we cannot change people's minds in a short space of time." Like all officials interviewed, Mr. Tu often speaks in set formulas as if from a manual. "Through 'patriotic education' the monks have learned 'what is not allowed' and 'what is illegal,'" he tells me.

Asked for clarification, he explains that monks teaching children is "not allowed." Monks demonstrating with pro-independence slogans is "illegal."

Mr. Tu dismisses stories of brutality and torture. "A person is responsible for his own law-breaking," he says calmly. "Our responsibility is to look after the great majority of [law-abiding] lamas."

The London-based Tibet Information Network says it knows of at least 210 monks and nuns still in jail for taking part in peaceful demonstrations over the past decade. Merely to shout a pro-independence slogan may earn a sentence of eight years. There are frequent stories—routinely denied by Beijing—of inmates being beaten with iron rods and electric batons. Several allegedly died during a protest at Drapchi prison in 1998.

Life seems more relaxed in Lhasa than during my last visit in 1994 when memories were fresh of pro-independence marches and the 1989 imposition of martial law. The Chinese military maintains a low profile, although Lhasa houses the massive headquarters of half a dozen different commands—from border guards to riot troops.

In the square before the Jokhang temple, where monks and nuns once marched, two bored policemen sit on chairs barking through a loudspeaker at anyone who pauses for too long.

Dalai Lama's Illness

No one now expects the intermittent dialogue between the Dalai Lama and Beijing since the early 1980s to produce results. A Beijing magazine this month has repeated the standard line that he can "return to the embrace of the motherland if he gives up his independence demand."

But asked if the Dalai will ever return, Mr. Tu replies contemptuously that "he has now sunk in the mud too deep to renounce all he has done in the past."

The Dalai Lama's nuanced proposals, made over the past 15 years, for Tibet to enjoy something short of independence are dismissed as insincere. His recent illness has also raised questions about the future in the event of his death. China would undoubtedly seek to control the choice of his next "reincarnation," as they did in 1995 after the death of the Panchen Lama, Tibet's second spiritual leader.

The new boy Panchen is now being educated in Beijing "in religious studies and science," it is said in Lhasa. He is being groomed to play a political role which could one day supplant the paramount status of the Dalai Lama.

Yet official statements have made it clear that the dominance of Buddhism in Tibet, however tightly controlled, is seen as a continuing threat to Chinese-led "stability." And that threat will only diminish if the economy of Tibet—still the poorest region of China—can finally be transformed.

Forbidden Practice[4]

By Juliet Rowan
Daily Yomiuri, May 25, 2002

"Truthfulness," "compassion" and "forbearance" don't seem like the kind of words that warrant arrest, but when a lone Frenchman unfurled a banner emblazoned with them in Beijing's Tiananmen Square earlier this month, Chinese authorities were quick to jump on him. That's because these terms represent the guiding principles of Falun Gong, the spiritual movement that amassed millions of followers before being abruptly banned in the country in 1999.

The arrest of the Frenchman, who was deported after about 24 hours in custody and forbidden to enter China for five years, came on the 10th anniversary of the movement. The incident served as yet another reminder of the Chinese government's unwillingess to alter its hardline stance against Falun Gong. Falun Gong (also known as Falun Dafa) dates back to 1992, with the publication of a complicated book by an obscure individual named Li Hongzhi. Li outlined a method for personal cultivation that combined elements of Buddhism, Taoism and traditional Qigong exercises. Released well into the post-Cultural Revolution era when China's citizens once again felt comfortable exploring their spirituality, the book quickly became a best-seller.

The tide began to turn, however, in 1998, when Li fled to New York after voicing suspicions that some in his country's government wanted him dead. In April the following year, 10,000 practitioners staged a protest in Beijing. Threatened by the scale of the gathering, the Chinese leadership branded Falun Gong "an evil cult" and promptly outlawed it, beginning an aggressive campaign to round up adherents.

According to the Web-based Falun Dafa Information Center, more than 100,000 practitioners have been arrested and illegally detained since the ban was imposed and more than 20,000 sent to government "reeducation" camps without trial. Reports of torture and abuse against practitioners in the camps and prisons have been widespread, sparking condemnation from world leaders and human rights groups like Amnesty International. The U.S. Congress has passed two resolutions calling for the release of jailed Falun Gong practitioners in China, the most recent being in July last year.

As of this week, the information center claims 410 practitioners have been killed by police brutality. The Chinese government denies knowledge of a single such incident.

Falun Gong's Li, meanwhile, has also been the target of criticism over suggestions he exerts undue pressure on practitioners to stage public protests in China, despite the likelihood of arrest and imprisonment.

Practitioners here in Japan vehemently deny the suggestions. "(Li) has never asked us to do anything," says Elsie Chang, a computer systems coordinator at a school in Tokyo who was arrested on Jan. 1, 2000, at a mass gathering in Tiananmen Square. "We feel that we have to help our fellow practitioners."

Shinly Shaw, a Chinese national who has lived and worked in Japan since 1996 and was detained in Beijing for a month after attending the same event as Chang, agrees. "Falun Gong is free will," she says. "The persecution is unreasonable and unjustified. It's the evil regime that should be criticized and stopped."

Falun Gong attracts practitioners from a wide range of backgrounds, many of whom encounter the practice almost by accident. Chang, who comes from Malaysia, was introduced to the teachings

---

Falun Gong attracts practitioners from a wide range of backgrounds, many of whom encounter the practice almost by accident.

---

by a Chinese roommate when she first came to Japan in 1998, while Takehiko Kanai, a 30-year-old accountant from Tokyo, became a practitioner after Li's book caught his attention in a bookstore about a year ago. "The book explained the true existence of the world," he says.

Neither Chang nor Kanai adhered to any form of organized religion or spiritual practice before.

According to the Falun Dafa Information Center, more than 100 million people in 40 countries practice Falun Gong. Most combine study of Li's teachings with tai chi-like exercises designed to stimulate energy flows in the body. Whether or not they choose to believe Li's sometimes unusual claims, including that elderly women will regain their menstrual period, practitioners say the physical benefits of the exercises are immense. "They make me feel warm and powerful and very concentrated," says Shaw, who credits the practice with ridding her of the frequent bouts of flu she suffered in the past.

For most, though, Falun Gong's greatest strength lies in its ability to bring about positive changes in one's character. "I used to be a very cynical person. I just complained about everything," Shaw, 34, says. "Now my first instinct in a conflict is to search my inner self for my own faults instead of finding fault with others or with my environment."

Chang, 35, echoes her sentiment. "I was the short-tempered one in my family," she says. "Even they noticed how calm I have become."

As in other parts of the world, Falun Gong practitioners in Japan display a strong commitment to fighting the persecution of their counterparts in China. They also strive to dispel negative images of Falun Gong as cultlike or beyond the reach of ordinary people— images they see as stemming from propaganda spread by the Chinese government.

Practitioners in Japan take turns maintaining a constant vigil in front of the Chinese Embassy in Tokyo. Many also spend weekends handing out leaflets to raise awareness of the persecution and the benefits of the practice itself. Marches are organized several times a year, with one held in Tokyo on May 12 to commemorate the 10th anniversary of Falun Gong attracting about 200 practitioners from places as far away as Hiroshima.

A considerable number of practitioners in Japan also go to China to make appeals—often at great cost. Kanai, who attended a rally by about 50 practitioners from various countries in Tiananmen Square in February, spent four days in the custody of local authorities before being allowed to return to Japan.

"We were taken to a hotel room, but there was nothing to sleep on. We just sat on the floor," he recalls. "The windows were blacked out and we had to go to the toilet in the same room. It wasn't sanitary."

Despite the personal hardship—Kanai also fasted for the duration of his confinement—he has no regrets about making the trip, saying he did it as a show of support for Chinese practitioners.

"If lots of practitioners from other countries go to China, Chinese practitioners will see that (such people) are able to practice (free of persecution) in their own countries," he says. "That's what I wanted to communicate."

Academic Freedom in China[5]

By Qinglian He
Academe, May/June 2002

China has never enjoyed real academic freedom, not even during more recent decades in which the government has carried out economic reform. The methods used to restrict free expression—most of which are unknown by Western scholars—have, however, changed over the past twenty years as a result of more openness in China to outside influences and a growing willingness among the Chinese people to question their government.

The worst time for Chinese scholars was during the era of Mao Zedong, from 1949 to 1976, when the Chinese government conducted a campaign of brainwashing intellectuals. If one dared to criticize any policy or political leader, he or she could be prosecuted and sent to a labor camp or sentenced to life in prison or death. All intellectuals felt compelled to praise Mao and his regime; those who actually contributed to communist propaganda were rewarded by a higher position and salary.

In 1957 the Chinese regime labeled its cultural and academic policy "Cultivating Thousands of Flowers and Encouraging Hundreds of Voices." But the so-called thousands of flowers and hundreds of voices did not have anything to do with freedom of speech or academic research; instead, the slogan was intended to encourage praise of the totalitarian system in China through various means, from poem, novel, and movie to drama.

Have market-oriented reforms and increased receptiveness to the outside world brought about academic freedom for Chinese intellectuals? Superficially, one may say yes. In contrast with Mao's era, Chinese intellectuals can read the literature of western social sciences, and, as long as they don't directly criticize the regime, they can use the research approaches of the social sciences. In addition, they can enjoy reading classical Chinese literature and Russian and Soviet literature. All of these materials were prohibited between the mid-1960s and mid-1970s, during the Cultural Revolution.

Less restriction does not, however, suggest that the current regime allows real academic freedom. There are still many areas that academics cannot touch. For example, intellectuals are not permitted to introduce or study western political systems or democracy; research on the Cultural Revolution and the history of the Chinese

---

Communist Party is restricted; and reform policies "should" be evaluated only in a positive way, that is, studies of them "should not" be biased against official positions.

Under China's constitution, a doctrine called "four principles," which insists on the dictatorship of the party, dominates all cultural and academic activities. Moreover, in China's political system, such activities are monitored regularly by the party's propaganda departments, whose function is to monitor culture and academia and give orders about what cannot be discussed. Anyone who goes a little beyond the limits set by the departments may face penalties. The system penetrates every corner of society; there are departments from the central regime to the county level, from the Chinese Academy of Social Sciences to each university and research institute.

As Chinese society has gradually opened to outside influences, the government has had to develop more sophisticated means of ideological control than it used in Mao's era. As recently as about ten years ago, after the Tiananmen Massacre, the regime was still relying on its traditional methods. It published articles in official newspapers and distributed documents smearing students who demonstrated for democracy and dissidents exiled abroad, and it forced everyone in China to discuss these official materials and to show their loyalty to the regime.

The regime is learning that the Chinese people are no longer naive; they want to find the truth.

Such methods have becomes less and less effective, however, and sometimes they completely fail. As more people make independent judgments and decline to defame those who are labeled as "enemies of the state" or who are penalized by the regime, political persecution of intellectuals often results in what the government dislikes: the intellectuals actually gain more social reputation, respect, and influence. The regime is learning that the Chinese people are no longer naive; they want to find the truth.

Another factor forcing the government to change its ways is criticism from the international community regarding human rights in China. As a result of consistent international pressure, the regime has moved to improve its image by adjusting its policy on ideological control. Penalties are no longer the only instruments applied; more "carrots" are now offered. The carrots are usually economic incentives and academic "reputation."

Cooperative intellectuals see their salaries raised. Government offices select "distinguished scholars," who receive special subsidies; promotion in academic careers becomes much easier as more of these senior positions are distributed. The Ministry of Education honors politically loyal followers by appointing them as instructors in Ph.D. programs, whether or not they are qualified. The government makes research funds available to professors who follow official policy and doctrines. Favored members of educational organizations and research institutes get opportunities to visit abroad. Universities are even allowed to "sell" master's or Ph.D. degrees to make money. One can pay a huge amount of money to join a program without exams, take several low-level courses, submit a paper written by somebody else, and receive a diploma from a distinguished university. "Carrots" are indeed attractive.

"Sticks" are used in a hidden, if not secretive, way. Penalties such as being fired or having one's articles or books banned are no longer announced through formal official documents. Instead, orders for such penalties are now given orally, either over the phone or face to face. Moreover, when such orders are sent down from the top, they are always followed by these instructions: do not take any notes, make any recordings, or ask which office has issued the orders; simply memorize them. When asked to explain why it applies such "secret" methods, the government usually says that it doesn't want the intellectuals being punished to gain social reputation from the penalties. Actually, its purpose is to hide its actions from international human rights organizations.

The penalties take various forms. A slight one stops a promotion that an academic deserves. In China, salary, housing, and medical care are linked with seniority, so someone who gets such a penalty may encounter difficulties. A more severe penalty may involve being laid off. Once someone is laid off for political reasons, it would be hard for the person to find another formal job, because no university or research institute wants to invite trouble by hiring a person the regime has defined as having a "political spot." A research fellow at the Chinese Academy of Social Sciences, Xiaoya Chen, suffered such a fate. In the early 1990s she wrote an academic book titled *History of the June Fourth Political Movement*, which touched on the most sensitive research topic in China: the democratic movement of 1989. She was immediately fired. She has been unemployed for about ten years now and has to struggle to survive without income or housing of her own. The most terrifying penalty the regime imposes against independent intellectuals is to put them under surveillance by the state security police. This penalty is often applied to intellectuals who criticize government policies or uncover evidence of corruption.

In recent years, the regime has developed a new strategy of political persecution. It no longer charges people with criticizing the government. Instead, it accuses them of taking bribes or of engaging in "economic crime." The latest case took place in Shanxin Province last fall. A journalist, Qinrong Gao, wrote about corruption in the provincial government and was arrested and charged with economic crime. Espionage or "threatening state security" are other charges that have become familiar to westerners. The regime keeps such charges secret when it imposes them against intellectuals inside China who have a high social reputation or those who visit China from abroad, particularly from the United States.

The efforts of the Chinese regime to control intellectuals extend to its treatment of western scholars who study China. The government selectively invites as visiting scholars those who praise the policies of the Chinese government, giving them information about opportunities to conduct research in China. Scholars who have published criticism of the regime are, however, considered "unfriendly to China" and may see their visa applications rejected without explanation.

The careers of many western scholars of China depend on their conducting fieldwork in the country, leading some to maintain a "good" relationship with the regime by restricting their research programs to topics the government favors and avoiding criticism of government policies. Not all scholars are willing to apply such a strategy to get access to China. Some who have declined to do so have faced pressure for not being able to do research in China. As a result of its approach to western academics, the Chinese government has been quite successful in influencing images of China's current situation in western scholarship.

Since Mao's era, the method of controlling intellectuals and academic activities in China has moved from "hard and bloody" tactics to "soft and hidden" ones. The new approach is to encourage the "voluntary cooperation" of intellectuals with the regime. Reliance on such "cooperation" can be found in many other countries. What is so disturbing about China is that the regime's "marketization under dictatorship" is often identified both in and outside China as a progressive process that is superior to democratization efforts in the former Soviet Union and eastern European countries. In terms of academic freedom, however, the process has hardly been progressive. The Chinese government may have improved its image in the eyes of the world, but it has continued its tradition, albeit in a less visible way, of restricting free expression.

SAR Must Stand True to Its Words[6]

BY JASPER BECKER
SOUTH CHINA MORNING POST, APRIL 20, 2002

When exiled Chinese dissident Harry Wu Hongda was refused entry into Hong Kong on Monday, it was another blow to the territory's traditional role as a sanctuary for free speech in the Chinese world.

It coincided with the hosting of the largest literature festival ever staged in Hong Kong, an important effort to recast the city's role in a new form.

The second Standard Chartered International Literary Festival, which ends tomorrow, has brought together about 60 writers. The common thread is that although they write in English, they have Asian roots.

Although the festival is not about Chinese literature, and did not include many mainland writers, the organisers did manage to attract big names from the world of exiled dissident writers, like Yang Lian and Huang Beiling.

Inevitably, discussions come around to what kind of role Hong Kong can play as it draws closer to Beijing.

Mr. Wu angrily claimed his expulsion showed Hong Kong's "one country, two systems" concept was already over.

Ever since the "100 days of reform" was crushed in the last years of the 19th century, Hong Kong, like other treaty ports, has served as a sanctuary for writers and politicians who fell out of favour with the powers that be.

Communist Party members made full use of this during the 1930s, '70s and '80s, when Hong Kong was a conduit for dissidents and for information as various factions fought for power.

If that changes, Hong Kong will lose its unique importance in the Chinese world. Its relevance will diminish in parallel with its threatened pre-eminence as the world's foremost trade and finance centre.

"Hong Kong is still the only place to keep media freedom," said Huang Beiling, the poet who founded *Tendency*, the literary journal for exiles. In August 2000, he was arrested for illegally publishing his journal on the mainland.

Speaking soon after Harry Wu was deported, Huang said: "I still worry that in a few years I will not be able to get in."

Hong Kong still has a chance to position itself as the market place for Chinese arts and literature before the mantle is grabbed by another city.

Taipei made a first stab at the title last September when it hosted the first Taiwan International Literature Festival and tried to bring together some big names from the mainland and abroad.

The effort foundered because mainland writers refused to come, and the star attraction, Caribbean Nobel Prize winner Derek Walcott, could not attend because the event took place just days after the September 11 terrorist attacks in the United States.

With generous government support, cities such as Singapore and Kwangju, in South Korea, have also been organising arts festivals. It will not be long before mainland cities also try to get involved.

China has never before hosted an international literature festival, but with the 2008 Olympics on the horizon, it seems more than likely it will try.

So far, Hong Kong still has great advantages over any mainland city with regard to the freedom publishers enjoy. They do not, for instance, have to obtain a government permit to print and distribute books.

Yet this relative advantage could change, although it does seem

---

Dissident avante garde artists who were once arrested for staging illegal exhibitions are now openly exhibiting and selling their works on the mainland.

---

unlikely at the moment. But take a look at what is happening with fine arts on the mainland.

Dissident avante garde artists who were once arrested for staging illegal exhibitions are now openly exhibiting and selling their works on the mainland. Several cities, including Shanghai, are vying to host international art exhibitions at official museums. The state is not quite so afraid of the loss of control over what people paint or sculpt as it used to be.

"They are more afraid of words," said Yang, one of the so-called "misty poets" attacked during the 1983 anti-spiritual pollution campaign.

Huang Feng helps run an underground poetry magazine on the mainland and was arrested in 2000 when he spoke out against the arrest of his brother. "Last year was the most difficult time since Tiananmen," he said.

Huang Feng says authorities have closed several publications and banned many books.

One such book was written by the poet Liao Yiwu, a collection of reportage gathered from the "lower depths".

One story was an interview with a Taiwanese businessman who consumed female foetuses to boost his potency.

The state clearly still feels threatened by literature, even if it is not overtly political. It is also sensitive about works by the diaspora of writers who fled abroad after 1989. Yet the reality is that their importance inside China faded some time ago.

> *Sooner or later, Chinese literature is likely to break free from the restrictions.*

Poets like Yang became famous in quite a different era, when, for a brief period, underground and experimental literature became the mainstream.

"Poets were treated like pop stars in the early 1980s," says Professor Mabel Lee, the Australian translator and academic.

Poetry readings were attended by large numbers of students and gained attention from the security apparatus. These days, few people read difficult poetry and poets are considered less subversive than they might seem to be.

No one is quite sure how many writers are in jail in China, but it is likely their numbers are less than a dozen or so.

Even that is bad enough and shows how much politics and literature remain tangled up in the minds of China's rulers. Yet, at the same time, the reality shows writing is well on its way to becoming commercialised.

There are even large numbers of pirate printers who sell vast quantities of any book in demand. Even though Nobel prize winner Gao Xingjian cannot publish his works officially in China, they are nonetheless available.

Official policies on the arts have yet to come to terms with the reality of the market. Early this year, President Jiang Zemin took a hard line when he addressed a national congress on writers and artists.

Writers like Huang Beiling and Yang feel indignant about both aspects of contemporary China: the crude censorship and the crass commercialism.

Yang cites the huge advance given to a book written by the ex-girl-friend of Gu Cheng, the misty poet who went to New Zealand. He killed himself and his wife, and now the mistress is trying to exploit the tragedy.

What is more, they feel writers in China are failing to write about what is really going on because they too willingly censor themselves and avoid sensitive topics. At the same time, exiled writers are cut off from opportunities to do so.

Yang talks angrily about what has happened to friends who stayed behind, became rich and now support the status quo.

"They don't feel any shame. A former writer friend told me: 'Whoever is against the Communists is now against me,'" he said.

Yet sooner or later, Chinese literature is likely to break free from the restrictions.

Some time soon, China will be keen to bring top international writers back home. Many came in the early 1980s but stayed away from Tiananmen.

Western readers will be keen to see more of Chinese mainstream writing other than memoirs or dissident-style literature as the nation's presence is increasingly felt on the international stage.

For the moment, festival organisers are unable to invite non-official writers and seem reluctant to put on stage the official delegations of safe hacks who will not bring in the public.

Yang thinks the mainland has become a cultural desert, with people just obsessed with making money—and that provides a chance for Hong Kong.

"Funnily enough, that is just what we used to say about Hong Kong in the 1980s," he said. "Now I think this is the one place you can still talk about all kinds of other things."

IV. U.S.-Chinese
Relations

Editor's Introduction

When President Richard Nixon first set foot in China on February 21, 1972, he was warmly greeted by Chou En-Lai, the Chinese premier and foreign minister. In his book *In the Arena: A Memoir of Victory, Defeat and Renewal* (1990), Nixon recalled that Chou told him, "Your hand-shake came over the vastest ocean in the world—twenty-five years of no communication." At the conclusion of Nixon's visit on February 27, 1972, the United States and China issued a joint statement known as the Shanghai Communiqué. While both nations acknowledged their differences over several key issues, the United States and China pledged to normalize relations, respect each other's sovereignty, settle disputes peacefully, and work to reduce the danger of military conflict. In 1979 the United States and China established full diplomatic relations, and since then, the two nations have dealt with each other cordially, for the most part. The writers in this section discuss China's relationship with the United States today, identifying issues of mutual cooperation and sources of tension.

In the *Los Angeles Times*, Jay Taylor writes that President George W. Bush has quietly revised the "one China" policy of his six predecessors. Under that policy, the United States recognized China and Taiwan, which seeks to keep its political independence from the mainland, as one nation. However, the United States has sold arms, including advanced weapons, to Taiwan and expressed hope that China and Taiwan could resolve their differences peacefully, which many analysts interpret as a warning to China not to use military force against Taiwan. According to Taylor, the Bush administration has made it clear that the United States will do "whatever it takes"—even use nuclear weapons—to defend Taiwan, a policy that has threatened the future of U.S.-Chinese relations.

In an article from the *South China Morning Post*, Simon Pritchard discusses how and why relations between the United States and China improved after the terrorist attacks of September 11, 2001. Although relations between the two nations had become strained after the "spy plane incident" in April 2001, with September 11 and the start of the war in Afghanistan, Pritchard observes that President Bush found China an unlikely ally in the struggle against terrorism. In addition, while the economies of many nations lagged in 2001, China's economy remained robust and attracted American investors. According to Pritchard, both the American war against terrorism and economic factors have brought the United States and China back together, at least for the time being.

Dean Calbreath's article from the *San Diego Union-Tribune* reports that many foreign policy analysts and experts in the United States are unsure of how to deal with China. As an example, Calbreath describes a meeting in 2001 of the U.S.-China Security Review Commission, a bipartisan group of 12 experts that was established by Congress to discuss the United States' policy toward China but which failed to reach a consensus. Calbreath suggests that the commission, like the United States itself, is hampered in its understanding of China by insufficient intelligence and primary resources, including Chinese military newspapers that have yet to be translated into English and subscriptions to just a few of the periodicals published by Beijing's military think tanks.

Kenneth R. Timmerman's article from *Insight* examines efforts by the United States to resume military ties with China that had been severed in April 2001 after the spy plane incident between the two countries. Timmerman reports that the United States was willing to resume a dialogue and re-open military channels with China, but only if the United States enjoyed the same benefits from them as China did. Timmerman describes how steps were made towards this reciprocity in late June 2002.

Gregg Jones of the *Dallas Morning News* addresses another area of contention between the United States and China: President Bush's decision to deploy a missile defense shield. Although Bush has insisted that the shield will protect the United States and its allies from missile attacks from "rogue" states, such as Iran, Iraq, Libya, and North Korea, China fears that the shield's protection may be extended to Taiwan. Jones explains that the Chinese "contend that any missile shield would badly damage U.S.-Chinese relations, backing China into a strategic corner by rendering its small nuclear arsenal useless as a counterweight to American might."

The final article in this section is a lengthy interview with President Jiang Zemin that was conducted in 2001 by the *New York Times*. In this interview, Jiang reiterates his belief in amicable U.S.-China relations; discusses his nation's view of an American missile defense shield and the conditions under which China would feel compelled to upgrade its military; comments on China's relationship with Taiwan; and considers his government's willingness to permit a more open society in the future.

Bush Scraps China Policy of Six Presidents[1]

By Jay Taylor
Los Angeles Times, April 28, 2002

Last year, with U.S. attention riveted on the Middle East and terrorism, the Bush administration quietly revised the "one China" policy of six previous presidents. Seeing China as our potential No.1 enemy, the Pentagon prepared the way for the United States to kill millions of Chinese, if necessary, to protect the separate status of Taiwan. Beijing is angry. But only a few months after this policy change was highlighted in the leaked *Nuclear Posture Review*, the administration is hosting Vice President Hu Jintao, the likely next president of China, this week in Washington. In either capital, does the left hand know what the right is doing?

Over the past year, one-China traditionalists in the administration successfully moved U.S.-China relations ahead, not the least because they were overwhelmingly supported by U.S. business and by the president's father. Economic ties between China and the United States continued to expand. The two countries closely cooperated on a range of issues, from Korea to terrorism, and Washington handled bilateral crises with patient diplomacy. As in the past, the U.S. government preferred jawboning to sanctions in pressing China to improve its human-rights record. For almost 30 years, creative ambiguity was at the heart of the one-China policy: The United States warned China not to use force to resolve the Taiwan issue but did not categorically pledge to defend the island regardless of Taiwan's position on sovereignty. The U.S. assured China that it would not support or recognize Taiwan's independence but, at the same time, continued shipping advanced weapons to the island for its self-defense. This balanced approach provided a framework for U.S.-China detente, for Taiwan's remarkable economic growth and democratization, and for the stunning expansion of cross-strait business, social, and cultural relations. Coupled with dramatic changes inside China, these developments also directly contributed to the opening of China's closed society. From Richard M. Nixon through Bill Clinton, U.S. administrations believed that the one-China policy would lead eventually to a peaceful agreement formalizing, in some loose manner, the unity of China and Taiwan, and that this would be in the U.S. interest.

---

1. Article by Jay Taylor from *Los Angeles Times* April 28, 2002. Copyright © Jay Taylor. Reprinted with permission.

But early on, the Bush administration made repeated categorical pledges to do "whatever it takes" to protect the island. The rationale behind this change was the belief among the Pentagon's top civilians that Taiwan is a strategic platform that must be denied to the emerging power of East Asia, the most dangerous potential rival to U.S. global preeminence. The administration declared that it still accepted the one-China principle, but it asserted as late as January that Taipei was free to reject the principle, as it has done since 1999.

While ending the ambiguity on Taiwan's defense, the administration has muddied the waters on the previously clear U.S. opposition to the island's independence. This switch was long advocated by leading revisionists on China, such as Deputy Defense Secretary Paul D. Wolfowitz and John Bolton, an undersecretary in the State Department. Evidence of the change is not hard to find. For the first time since 1978, the State Department last year permitted Taiwan's president, vice president and premier to hold separate meetings with U.S. lawmakers on American soil. Most recently, the Taiwan defense minister held a "non-official" meeting with Wolfowitz in Florida.

While ending the ambiguity on Taiwan's defense, the administration has muddied the waters on the previously clear U.S. opposition to the island's independence.

China protested these departures from the one-China policy as "hegemonic acts of gross interference." But Beijing has not threatened a major breakdown in relations, much less heightened tensions across the Taiwan Strait. China dearly wants to avoid any such crisis. Its booming economy depends in large part on America's continuing purchase of more than $80 billion in Chinese-made products and huge capital investments in China. Beijing puts great stock in hosting the 2008 Olympic Games, and nothing spoils an Olympics like a war or even a whiff of its possibility. Furthermore, a new Chinese leadership will be chosen in the fall, and the incumbent pragmatists, led by President Jiang Zemin, and the incoming ones, led by Hu, do not want a building sense of national grievance against the United States to play into the hands of the more conservative faction, which would be happy to exchange nationalism for prosperity as the main raison d'etre of the regime.

Meanwhile, China has substantially enhanced its prestige and influence in East Asia through diplomacy and, in some cases, financial aid. It does not want to see this trend upset by an upsurge in tensions in the strait. Almost certainly, the Peoples Liberation Army has urged the regime to delay any showdown over Taiwan.

Beijing may also believe that Taiwan's multiplying connections across the strait will advance the possibilities of a peaceful one-China resolution of Taiwan's status, whatever the revisionists may want. Today, more than 50,000 Taiwanese companies have more than $60 billion in investments on the mainland, more than 1 million Taiwanese visit the mainland each year, and 400,000 Taiwanese citizens live in Shanghai.

Finally, the Chinese leaders calculate that the struggle for President Bush's favor on the one-China issue is far from over. They know the president wants a constructive relationship with China and that many important interests and key individuals do not believe the United States should keep open the option of using Taiwan as a strategic base. Clearly, the Chinese don't want to undercut traditionalists like Secretary of State Colin L. Powell. So, Hu is coming to accentuate the positive.

Still, administration revisionists must take heart in the fact that Hu is in town. They have always contended that if the United States made clear its determination to defend Taiwan under any conceivable circumstance, China would live with it and eventually with Taiwan's independence. Hu's current visit, as well as Zemin's eagerness to stay at Bush's Texas ranch this fall, confirms this view, contends the revisionists.

They could be wrong, however. At some point, the Chinese people could feel so strongly about what they would see as the final violation of the unity of China that they would be willing to go to war. The revisionists, and those in the upper echelon of the Bush administration who apparently support them, notably Vice President Dick Cheney and Defense Secretary Donald H. Rumsfeld, no doubt have thought this war scenario through. They realize that with only 2% of the mainland's population, no matter how many F-16s, submarines, or anti-missile missiles we sell Taiwan, the island would not likely prevail in a prolonged conflict with China. A Chinese blockade, which few nations would challenge, could quickly devastate the Taiwan economy. Furthermore, the hawks understand that if the United States intervened in such a conflict, regardless of how many thousands of smart bombs it rained down on the mainland, China might outlast the patience of the American people.

That brings up the administration's *Nuclear Posture Review*, which, for the first time, declared that the deployment of U.S. nuclear weapons should take into account the possibility of a nuclear war with China "over Taiwan." In other words, to maintain a potential strategic offshore base for use in a hypothetical conflict with China, we may have to fight a nuclear war with China. This would be "a self-fulfilling prophecy" of biblical proportions.

Emperors' New Closeness[2]

By Simon Pritchard
South China Morning Post, February 20, 2002

Perhaps the most significant point about United States President George W. Bush's Asian tour is that he is here at all. America's European allies historically invoked the all-for-one article in their common defence pact after September 11, but it was Asia that a strategically focused U.S. administration graced first.

Much has been made of the raw power implications of U.S. military hegemony displayed in Afghanistan. The Bush presidency has become a war presidency as America warms to a political mission matching its muscle. Europeans wince at the moral simplicity of the "axis of evil" doctrine and feel marginalised. But where European multilateral instincts and institutions look out of sync with a results-focused U.S. presidency, Asia remains a melange of testy alliances and nervy self-interest. Central Asia represents a new theatre of U.S. military expansion. Japan and China account for the lion's share of the U.S. deficit in trade. Above all, the Asian polity remains dominated by state power and strategic calculations.

When Mr. Bush meets Chinese leaders in Beijing tomorrow and Friday, the two sides will find much to agree on. Beijing's diplomatic hand in forging an India-Pakistan detente and reported eavesdropping assistance on al-Qaeda bases suggest that "strategic competition" between the two Pacific superpowers may yield to stable engagement.

Any rapprochement has a temporary feel as distrustful competition between Washington and Beijing seems the long-run basis to the relationship. For now, the new realpolitik dictated by Washington's war on terrorism and Beijing's liking for a common enemy in the shape of "terrorists" in its western regions, justifying state action, means both sides have their planets in alignment.

It all looks different from last April, when the downed U.S. spy plane incident ruptured relations. A then-weak President Bush was focused on rolling back his predecessor's China engagement and attuned to the Republican Party's human rights-focused grassroots. Business interests, which were the strongest U.S. lobby group arguing for engagement, went quiet and the lustre was taken off China's expected World Trade Organisation (WTO) entry.

Subsequently, the economics of the relationship have flowed Beijing's way. Critically, fears of a post-September 11 economic implosion forged the consensus necessary to secure an agreement launching a new round of WTO trade liberalisation talks in November. Solidification of a developing country axis which had long felt marginalised was spurred by Beijing's WTO entry.

Above all, China has emerged as almost the only engine of growth in a recession-bound world economy. Contrary to immediate post-September 11 fears, globalisation and the trend of ruthless industrial outsourcing has not slowed. While developed economies were forced to roll forward the state following the terrorist attacks—bailing out airlines and cranking up spending—Beijing has maintained its breakneck reform effort, rolling back government from industries.

> *China has emerged as almost the only engine of growth in a recession-bound world economy.*

Beijing finds itself in the benign position of offering foreign business all the promise of market access to the world's fastest-growing economy with, as yet, little of the inevitable disappointment that must follow.

Thematic China stock investing is back in favour. U.S. multinationals are scouring Shanghai and Beijing for professional talent. Ahead of Mr. Bush's visit, official media has been blaring statistics showing the scale of U.S. investment and penetration in the mainland market. Splendid forecasts of phenomenal growth are back in fashion, with U.S. investment bank Lehman Brothers last week unfurling starry-eyed forecasts of the country's growth prospects.

The reality may be different. Moribund state-owned industries continue to shed staff into a dysfunctional social safety net and scandals such as that which emerged recently at the Bank of China show how far governance codes must improve. But a quick comparison with the predicament of Japan, where Mr. Bush began this week's trip, illustrates the momentum on Beijing's side.

Where presidents Jiang Zemin and Bush both deploy formidable executive power to respond to very different economic conditions, an embattled Prime Minister Junichiro Koizumi struggles to enact even mild reform to Japan's perilous economy.

For now, China seems to be rewriting the economic law of "comparative advantage" that says countries can only specialise in particular industries, by winning dominance in a multitude of industrial sectors to the detriment of other Asian economies.

Such industrial imperialism is rapidly altering the regional balance of economic power. Equally, U.S. consumers become more dependent daily on product supply chains linked to China's production heartlands. While Mr. Bush's visit will see hard-nosed debate on agriculture, looser restrictions on U.S. high-technology exports and anti-dumping issues, the economics for now seem mutually beneficial.

In an environment dominated by strategic imperatives and fears of a Japanese financial panic, Beijing appears a pillar of stability. As the U.S. again moves towards deficit economics and foreign private sector capital flows into its sluggish economy, the U.S. will become increasingly dependent on Beijing recycling U.S. dollars, earned from its huge trade surpluses, back into Treasury securities.

Such economic interdependence can galvanise stability. Yet when set against a backdrop of distrust, the same reliance can be destabilising, as seen in the inter-war years of the 1920s and 1930s, when beggar-thy-neighbour economics and nationalist ambition wrought chaos.

It should be remembered that within a year of winning the Gulf War in 1991, former president George Bush Sr. was in Japan demanding improved market access for U.S. producers. A bad economy and rising unemployment meant U.S. popular concerns quickly turned back to bread-and-butter matters.

For now, the U.S. fiscal reflation effort and its war on terrorism seem entwined. Military spending is rising and popular support for the administration's strategic aims remains sky-high.

That all bodes well for Beijing, which prefers its relations at a state-to-state level, rather than bogged down by the special interests of foreign democratic electorates. So long as Mr. Bush remains in war mode and the U.S. economy holds up, the new status quo looks likely to hold a while longer.

U.S. Strains to Understand China[3]

By Dean Calbreath
San Diego Union-Tribune, September 4, 2001

As lawmakers ducked out of town last month to flee the swelter-
ing humidity, a congressionally appointed panel met near the Capitol to tussle over what could be the century's stickiest foreign
policy problem: how to deal with the People's Republic of China.

Twenty witnesses filed into a hearing room in the Dirksen Senate
Office Building. They offered extremely conflicting views of the
world's largest nation.

Business executives marveled at the size of China's market.
Labor leaders complained about its low-wage competition. Army
officers and academics sparred over how much of a threat is posed
by the People's Liberation Army. Economists debated whether
China's economy will outstrip the United States' or collapse into
dust. When it was all over, panel member James Lilley, who served
as U.S. ambassador to Beijing during the 1989 Tiananmen Square
demonstrations, was sputtering with exasperation.

"You hear people talking ad nauseam about our relationship with
China and getting it wrong, wrong, wrong," said Lilley, one of six
Republicans sitting on the 12-member U.S.-China Security Review
Commission.

"What is China? A threat, a friend, a place of great potential or a
potential disaster zone? A great deal of damage can be done if you
get that question wrong."

Michael Ledeen, another Republican appointee, worried that
"nobody's smart enough to know how China's going to look in five
or ten years. We don't even have a proper model for China because
we've never seen anything like China."

The confusion mirrors the national debate over how to treat
China: engage it as an economic partner, contain it as a military
threat or find some happy medium—"congagement," as Washington's wordsmiths put it.

The debate has riven the Bush administration, with the State
Department leaning more toward engagement as the Defense
Department focuses on potential conflict in Asia, with a particular
emphasis on China and North Korea.

"State gets paid to negotiate toward a common ground. Defense
exists to fight battles and not compromise," said Larry Wortzel, a
former military attache in Beijing.

Michael Pillsbury, a specialist in Chinese affairs with the National Defense University, said one stumbling block to U.S. policy is that the government is so uninformed about China.

> *One stumbling block to U.S. policy is that the government is so uninformed about China.*

"Very few people who work on Chinese security matters can read Chinese well enough to stand in front of you, pick up a newspaper and read an article published by the Chinese military," Pillsbury told the security review commission.

Pillsbury said 98 percent of Chinese military newspapers are not translated into English. He complained that the U.S. government subscribes to a mere handful of the periodicals published by Beijing's military think tanks.

"The state of information from China is atrocious. It's ghastly," said commission member June Teufel Dreyer, a Sinologist at the University of Florida.

Dreyer, who recently conducted a review of Chinese documents at the Library of Congress, said much of the material is "a random collection of books or magazines discarded by the CIA. They aren't even filed. They're heaped in bunches."

With little unvarnished information available, legislators and bureaucrats often rely on lobbyists to help them sort out the complexities of Chinese relations.

The Blue Team

In recent years, the dominant voice on China has come from Fortune 500 companies and industry associations with financial stakes there. Last month's hearings were jammed with officials from the Electronics Industry Alliance, the Aerospace Industries Association, the National Cattlemen's Beef Association and the American Soybean Association pressing for more access to China's market.

"There's an old saying that if trade doesn't flow across international borders, armies will," said Henry Jo Von Tungeln, chairman of U.S. Wheat Associates.

Not all pressure groups take such a sanguine view of Chinese trade. One of the most active voices in the China debate has been the Blue Team, a loose-knit group of legislative aides, academics and former intelligence officers who see Beijing as a malevolent dictatorship on a hostile collision course with the United States.

Launched in 1998, the Blue Team grew out of the Project for the New American Century, a think tank backed by Pittsburgh billionaire Richard Mellon Scaife. At the time, Scaife was financing projects to embarrass Bill Clinton. He was, for instance, the key backer of the Arkansas Project, which dug up dirt on Clinton's sexual peccadilloes.

The name for the Blue Team—coined by William Triplett, a former China analyst for the CIA—comes from Chinese war games in which a Red Team represents the People's Liberation Army and the enemy is Blue. But in the beginning, the Blue Team concentrated as much fire on the White House as on Beijing.

In the book *The Year of the Rat*, for example, Triplett and fellow Blue Teamer Edward Timperlake accused Clinton of kowtowing to "Chinese arms dealers, spies, narcotics traffickers, gangsters, pimps, accomplices to mass murder, communist agents and other undesirables."

> *The Bush administration remains conflicted about China.*

Although the team has always been small, with as few as 40 or 50 members, it widened its influence through access to Scaife's publishing houses and positions on key congressional committees. Triplett, Timperlake and several other Blue Teamers worked as staff members for Republican legislators on Capitol Hill.

The Blue Team takes credit for helping draft some anti-China legislation, such as the Taiwan Security Enhancement Act, as well as spearheading Rep. Christopher Cox's probe into China's acquisition of U.S. technology. Blue Teamer Richard Fisher worked on Cox's staff.

"They were just trying to throw whatever mud they could at the administration and see what stuck," said former Clinton trade official Stephen Reinsch, who was attacked by the Blue Team as being too lax over U.S. high-tech exports to China.

Observers say the team's chief effect was to politicize the China debate. When academics or diplomats proposed stronger ties with China, Blue Teamers attacked them as "the Red Team," "panda huggers" or even paid agents of Beijing.

Reinsch, a Democratic appointee to the U.S.-China Security Review Commission, said the Blue Team wasn't alone.

"A lot of people in both the United States and China have an interest in making matters worse rather than better," he said.

"There's clearly an element in the People's Liberation Army that sees the U.S. as an evil hegemony, saying China needs to be prepared for the inevitable military conflict. And there's also a group in the U.S. that views China the same way. Our main goal should be to ensure that neither group gains the upper hand."

"Strategic Ambiguity"

Although the Blue Team has quieted since Bush's inauguration, some of its members have taken key roles in the administration's policy involving China.

Bush's arms control policy, for instance, is overseen by John Bolton, an executive of the conservative American Enterprise Institute whose name has been linked with the Blue Team. Bolton has pushed for U.S. diplomatic recognition of Taiwan, arguing that "the notion that China would actually respond with force is a fantasy."

Yet the Bush administration remains conflicted about China.

Deputy Secretary of Defense Paul Wolfowitz, Deputy Secretary of State Richard Armitage and Lewis Libby, Vice President Dick Cheney's chief of staff, for instance, want to end the U.S. policy of "strategic ambiguity" in support of Taiwan. But they have been rebuffed by National Security Adviser Condoleezza Rice and other officials who fear the tensions such a move might create.

To help resolve such issues, Congress set up the China Security Review Commission this spring. But the commission is also torn.

Among the Republican members are Arthur Waldron, a former strategist from the U.S. Naval War College who hopes China's regime will be driven from power; Stephen Bryen, who wants to sell more arms to Asian allies to counter China; and Ledeen, an Iran-contra figure who was known in the 1980s for floating the since-disproven rumor that the KGB was behind the attempted assassination of Pope John Paul II.

Democrats include Richard D'Amato, a former attache to the U.S. Embassy in Beijing who took part in Clinton's arms control initiatives; George Becker, an AFL-CIO official concerned about how cheap imports are affecting American labor; and Reinsch, the former Clinton trade official once targeted by the Blue Team.

"It's going to be quite a chore to come up with a consensus," said commission member Dreyer.

Many observers forecast that after much debate, the commission will probably recommend a policy not much different from Clinton's: bolstering economic ties with China while keeping a wary eye on its military.

"We have to stop talking about all this stuff that makes the headlines: missile defense, reunification with Taiwan," said former ambassador Lilley, who once advocated selling arms to Beijing under the former Bush administration. "We have to have a multifaceted relationship that is aware of all the dangers but still emphasizes markets, economics and trade."

Not that Lilley is an optimist about the market's effect on China.

"You hear all this BS from businessmen saying the Chinese are becoming freer and freer as the market opens up," he said. "And then you hear people say China's squeezing us blind with slave labor and using the money to buy new weapons from Russia to destroy us."

Lilley said what is needed is proper management of economic forces "to create a situation where the military option is less feasible.

"And that includes letting them know if they do screw around with missiles, we'll blow their heads off."

Rumsfeld Demands China Reciprocity[4]

By Kenneth R. Timmerman
Insight, July 15, 2002

Military ties between the United States and the People's Republic of China (PRC) came screeching to a halt in April 2001 when the Chinese air force attacked a U.S. Navy EP-3E surveillance aircraft in international airspace and forced it to land on Hainan Island in China. But now, 14 months later, the Bush administration has agreed to dispatch Assistant Secretary of Defense Peter Rodman to Beijing to revive those ties at a time when the PRC appears increasingly isolated and its much-touted strategic alliance with Russia may be on the rocks.

In remarks released prior to the trip, Deputy Defense Secretary Paul Wolfowitz said Rodman was going "to talk about the principles on which we can get our military-to-military relationship on a more solid framework, which will be of mutual benefit." A Pentagon spokesman, Lt. Cmdr. Jeff Davis, added that Rodman would be seeking Chinese assurances of "transparency, consistency and reciprocity" before the United States would consider restoring the military-exchange program.

The spark for the Rodman trip came during a sharp exchange at the Pentagon on May 1 between Secretary of Defense Donald Rumsfeld and visiting Chinese Vice President Hu Jintao over China's nuclear and missile proliferation. "Rumsfeld said we are perfectly willing to have contacts with you, but only if we get as much out of it as you do," a defense official tells *Insight*. Ultimately, the Rodman visit could lead to a restoration of the annual Defense Consultative Talks (DCT), a high-level meeting that formalizes a schedule of military-to-military exchanges for the coming year, if the Chinese agree to transparency and reciprocity. "But that's a big if—a huge if," the official says. "We hope the Chinese don't think Rodman is carrying the DCT in his hip pocket, because he's not."

U.S. critics question the timing of the announcement and its intent. "I'm not in favor of these contacts," defense consultant Stephen Bryen tells *Insight*. "The military exchanges with China are a one-way street. We give away stuff and the Chinese promise to behave, and these exchanges are being organized in the middle of a Chinese missile buildup that threatens Taiwan and the U.S.

---

4. Article by Kenneth R. Timmerman from *Insight* July 15, 2002. Copyright © *Insight*. Reprinted with permission.

fleet. It's amazing to me that the Bush people, who know better, would pursue a course the Clinton people invented." Bryen is a former deputy undersecretary of defense and a member of the congressionally mandated U.S.-China Security Review Commission, which during the last 18 months has been assessing U.S. policy goals and options. The commission will release an 11-chapter report in July that will include a series of "concrete proposals" aimed at better controlling the sale of strategic technology, commission members tell *Insight*.

Larry Wortzel, Asia policy analyst at the Heritage Foundation and a commission member, tells *Insight* that he favors a military-to-military dialogue with Communist China as "a component of our foreign policy," but that the content needs to be closely focused. "We need to have exchanges on things such as freedom of navigation, international airspace, proliferation, China's military buildup against Taiwan and how the PRC might create a threat that under the Taiwan Relations Act could oblige the United States to get into a conflict against China to defend Taiwan."

Neither Wortzel nor Bryen believe the United States should engage in the type of open-door policy toward the Chinese military that became a hallmark of the Clinton administration, when PRC generals and intelligence officers were invited into the heart of the U.S. defense establishment. "The Clinton people took a hell of a risk by letting them into our military facilities and inviting them to participate in our military exercises," Bryen says. "The Chinese look at it as a spying operation, which I believe it was."

But inviting the PRC military to visit top-secret U.S. bases, ballistic-missile submarines and joint-forces operations does not appear to be the Bush administration's intent, at least for now. Indeed, administration envoy Rodman, who headed the State Department's Office of Policy Planning during the George H. W. Bush administration and has worked in White House jobs under four Republican presidents, was a stern critic of Beijing's aggressive behavior toward Taipei and of PRC weapons sales to Middle East trouble spots before returning to government last year from his position as head of strategic studies at the Nixon Center for Peace and Freedom in Washington.

So why bother approaching the PRC at all? One reason may be to calm Chinese nerves as the United States gears up for a future battle with Iraq. "The Chinese responded very badly to Sept. 11," says professor Stephen Blank of the U.S. Army War College in Carlisle, Pa. "The day of the attack on America, a Chinese delegation was in Kabul to sign a trade agreement with the Taliban. Afterward, they publicly expressed doubt at U.S. accusations that al-Qaeda was behind Sept. 11 and demanded that the U.S. refrain from any unilateral response that was not sanctioned by the United Nations."

Chinese Internet chat rooms exploded with anti-American comments on Sept. 11, and the Beijing government pointedly refused to order flags on government buildings to be flown at half-mast. "Our response wasn't even as warm as Cuba's," a Chinese government foreign-policy analyst told the *Washington Post* on Sept. 14. Beijing was hoping it could capitalize on Sept. 11 by winning U.S. backing for its own efforts to crush a growing Uighur Muslim separatist movement in East Turkistan (Xinjiang). That support never came. Instead, the Chinese were caught off-guard by the way nations around the world rallied behind President George W. Bush and felt increasingly isolated, Blank and other analysts believe.

Beijing's failure to back the United States also weakened PRC credibility in the eyes of the Russians, who were looking for a partner to help combat the Taliban because of its support for anti-Russian separatists in Chechnya. "Sept. 11 destroyed the deal between China and Russia," Blank argues, "by revealing the misgivings many Russians were already feeling toward Beijing. [Russian President Vladimir] Putin saw that he could not rely on the Chinese to fight terrorism. The Chinese exposed themselves as weak and unavailable. As the Chinese proverb has it: 'Distant water cannot quench nearby fire.'"

The Chinese were caught off-guard by the way nations around the world rallied behind President George W. Bush.

The recently signed Sino-Russian strategic-cooperation agreement called for the two sides to use military force to aid each other in the event one was attacked [see "China and Russia Align against U.S.," Aug. 13, 2001]. "Even before the pact was signed, you had Russian Defense Minister Sergei Ivanov publicly worrying that the PRC would use the mutual-assistance clause to start something in Taiwan to get Russia involved in a fight it doesn't want," Blank says. "Sept. 11 made it clear the Chinese had nothing concrete to offer Russia in Central Asia."

Another motivator for Rodman's trip is to calm Chinese fears of the dramatic U.S.-Russian rapprochement that has resulted from the Bush-Putin relationship. Contrary to the dire predictions of the arms-control lobby, which for decades has claimed that the Anti-Ballistic Missile Treaty of 1972 was the "cornerstone" of strategic stability, President Bush demonstrated that the United States could withdraw from the treaty without starting a war. The decision actually has enhanced security, not reduced it. "Behind the scenes, the Bush administration told the Russians they could MIRV [multiple independent re-entry vehicle] their missiles if they felt uncomfortable with U.S. missile-defense plans," Blank tells *Insight*. "And so, in mid-June 2002, the Russians repudiated the second Strategic Arms Limitation Treaty [START II], which the U.S. never ratified. This allows them specifically to put multiple warheads on their strategic missiles."

The Russian decision, and the Bush administration's missile-defense plans, have left Beijing in the lurch. "They feel weakened and surrounded," Wortzel agrees.

Yet another reason to resume a dialogue with the PRC's military is to warn the Chinese of dangerous misconceptions that potentially could lead to conflict. Michael Pillsbury, a Chinese linguist and defense analyst who has compiled two books of Chinese military writings for the Pentagon's Office of Net Assessment, told the U.S.-China Commission last year that senior Beijing strategists, including Communist Party General Secretary Jiang Zemin, believe they can create secret weapons known as the "assassin's mace" to give themselves a decisive advantage over the United States during any PRC assault on Taiwan.

"An assassin's mace weapon is something that is designed based on American vulnerabilities," Pillsbury said. "You study what would bring the Americans to their knees in a specific conflict, such as the American effort to . . . perhaps to defend Taiwan, and you make a list of the American strengths and weaknesses and you focus on the weaknesses in an attempt to develop so-called assassin's-mace weapons that will penalize the Americans at a key moment, and you, by the way, conceal these weapons. That's the heart of the assassin's-mace idea. It's not exposed until it's needed at a key moment on the battlefield."

Pillsbury found references to 15 such weapons in Chinese military writings. "They focus a great deal on aircraft carriers," he says. "It's a big topic in China. There's even an Internet Website where people put up suggestions about good ways to attack American aircraft carriers." Pillsbury then described a conversation he had with a Chinese general at a conference in the PRC in late 2000. "'You know, this is like James Bond.' I said, 'Really? What are you talking about? I don't understand.' He said, 'You know, in the James Bond movies, just when James Bond is almost dead, he pulls something out of his pocket and it kills "Odd Job" or someone. That's assassin's mace. That's a sha sho jian.'"

Also a potential assassin's mace are antisatellite weapons. Despite repeated warnings from the intelligence community during the Clinton administration that the PRC was seeking to acquire such weapons, the United States remained silent when a British company, Surrey Space Systems, signed a contract with the Beijing government in October 1998 to provide microsatellite technology.

"British Prime Minister Tony Blair even presided over the signing ceremony," says Richard Fisher, an analyst with the Jamestown Foundation who is completing a book-length study of Chinese military systems. "Less than two years later, in June 2000, the Chinese launched the first microsatellites built using this technology. When coupled to a mobile space-launch system, which they are in the process of developing, this gives them a potential antisatellite capability," Fisher tells Insight. The PRC unveiled the prototype of a solid-fuel mobile space-launch vehicle, the KT-1, at the Zhuhai Air Show in November 2000, Fisher added. (For more information on the air show, see *www.stormpages.com/jetfight/airshow.htm*.)

Beijing's ongoing military modernization and China's growing independence from its suppliers during the last two to three years is yet another cause of concern to the Bush administration. For Alexander Nemets, a Russian scholar who closely monitors Chinese-Russian military cooperation, there are increasing signs that the PRC has taken dramatic steps toward "technological independence" from Russia in several key areas, including military aircraft, jet engines, manned spacecraft and naval weaponry. "The Chinese are getting very close to independence in weapons production. If they succeed, China will be able to directly threaten the United States in just a few years," Nemets tells *Insight*.

Several new PRC weapons systems developed initially with Russia now are reaching the production phase, Nemets and other analysts say. These include:

- The J-11 fighter-bomber, an improved version of the Sukhoi-27 SK, that now is being assembled under license by Shenyang Aircraft Corp. "By the end of 2001," Nemets says, "only engines, radar and some avionics were coming from Russia." According to some reports, the Chinese may be contemplating upgrading the Shenyang production line to assemble the Su-30, an all-weather attack aircraft that would present an even greater threat to Taiwan.

- The J-10 fighter, which resembles a cross between an F-16 and Israel's now-abandoned Lavi, is approaching serial production at the Chengdu Aircraft Corp. The PRC air force has selected this indigenous fighter to replace its obsolete J-7 (MiG-21) and Q-5 attack aircraft. Initially it will be powered by Russian-built AL-31F turbofan engines, but Nemets and other analysts say there is evidence that the PRC is trying to build an indigenous version, perhaps with help from Ukraine, known as the "Kunlun." In May 2002, Nemets says, the Shenyang Jet Engine Research Institute finished development of a Kunlun prototype.

- The JH-7/FBC-1 long-range strike aircraft, a two-seat fighter-bomber similar to the Su-24 or the British Tornado. According to some reports, the PRC air force has rejected full-scale production of this aircraft because of its 1970s design, preferring instead to purchase Su-30 MKK aircraft from Russia. But according to Nemets and other analysts, full-scale production of a naval-strike version for the PRC navy is under way at the Xian Aircraft Co. To power this indigenous aircraft, the Chinese purchased an estimated 70-80 used F-4 engines from Rolls-Royce two years ago. The first 10 production aircraft flew in September 2001.

The political chill between Moscow and Beijing has done little to slow the flow of strategic technologies into new Chinese weapons systems, all the analysts interviewed by *Insight* for this article agree. The Russians continue actively to assist the Chinese in developing the nuclear 093 attack submarine, a Chinese version of the S-300 PMU-1 long-range missile-defense interceptor, solid-fuel strategic missiles including the DF-31 and its submarine-launched version, the JL-2, and dozens of other weapons systems. "In a number of areas, the Chinese are developing systems specifically designed to attack U.S. forces," says Wortzel of the Heritage Foundation.

Pillsbury agrees. He believes Beijing may have initiated military cooperation with Moscow specifically with Taiwan in mind. "The Chinese saw the kind of package—force package, as we would say—they need to develop to 'liberate' Taiwan even if the Americans help Taiwan, and they've been assembling it piece by piece, very carefully, very slowly and in a very un-American way."

The Chinese military is "making dramatic progress across the board," says Fisher, who recently returned from Taipei. "By 2005, a window opens where the PRC will have superiority in enough categories of weapons, and the military doctrine to deploy them in combined-forces operations, to tempt the Beijing leadership to launch a quick military attack against Taiwan in the belief that they can present the United States with a fait accompli that will prevent the U.S. from intervening. Starting in 2005, we are heading into a real danger zone in the Taiwan Strait. This is a crisis, and it is beginning now."

If the Bush administration wants to put a cap on the PRC's aggressive ambitions, a hard-nosed dialogue with the Chinese military might be one way to start. "If anyone can make a college try, it's Peter Rodman," Fisher says. "But I have no faith that the Chinese will comply with any of our demands for reciprocity or transparency. They'll simply laugh at us—or cheat."

China Wary of U.S. Plan for Missile-Defense Shield[5]

BY GREGG JONES
DALLAS MORNING NEWS, MAY 1, 2001

Ask anyone in China to name the biggest thorn in U.S.-Chinese relations, and the answer almost invariably is Taiwan, the U.S.-armed island claimed by China.

But in the offices of senior Chinese government officials, at influential research centers and on university campuses, there is a growing preoccupation with what many see as another ticking time bomb in the volatile relationship: the Bush administration's vow to build a missile-defense system for the United States and its friends.

President Bush is scheduled to unveil his plans for the system on Tuesday. But Chinese officials and scholars say the details don't matter. They contend that any missile shield would badly damage U.S.-Chinese relations, backing China into a strategic corner by rendering its small nuclear arsenal useless as a counterweight to American might.

"Missile defense increases Chinese suspicions of America's strategic intentions toward China," said Zhu Feng, director of the international security program at Peking University's School of International Studies. "If China's missile deterrence is neutralized, then China's national security is threatened. It will arouse a radical reaction."

U.S. advocates say the system is needed to defend Americans from "rogue states" such as North Korea, Iraq, Iran and Libya, which might have the capability to hit the United States with long-range missiles in the next few years.

Many Chinese government officials, scholars and diplomats, however, say the "national missile-defense" and "theater missile-defense" systems under U.S. consideration are aimed at least in part at China.

Taiwan's Role

They fear such a system would include Taiwan, which China claims as a breakaway province, and Japan, a historical rival.

"They are using North Korea as a camouflage to cover up their real motivation," said Sha Zukang, China's top arms negotiator. "This can be used against others, including China."

---

5. Article by Gregg Jones from the *Dallas Morning News* May 1, 2001. Copyright © *Dallas Morning News*. Reprinted with permission.

As a result, the Chinese government—in partnership with Russia—is waging a diplomatic offensive to block missile defense. On Saturday, in the latest broadside in the war for global public opinion, China, Russia and three Central Asian states issued a joint declaration attacking the U.S. plan.

"The U.S. has the sovereign right to defend itself," said Mr. Sha, director-general of the department of arms control and disarmament at China's Foreign Ministry. "We are just advising and telling the U.S. to please don't do it. It's not in your interests or the interests of the international community."

In his speech Tuesday, Mr. Bush is expected to explain how his plan will differ from a Clinton administration proposal to place 100 missile interceptors in Alaska. At best, deployment of any system will take several years, experts say.

That is little consolation to China, Chinese officials and scholars say.

Treaty in the Way

To deploy such a system, the United States would have to either amend the 1972 Anti-Ballistic Missile treaty signed with the former

---

Already, the perceived threat posed by a U.S. missile shield has spawned a "massive popular sentiment of nationalism" in China.—**David Kelly, Australian Defense Force Academy**

Soviet Union—something that Russia refuses to do—or discard the treaty—a step that China and other critics say would have terrible consequences for the world.

"The 1972 ABM treaty is the cornerstone for strategic stability," said Mr. Sha. "[U.S. officials] have been telling us that for so many years. Now if you remove the cornerstone, the whole building will collapse. It will lead to an arms race. And it will lead to the proliferation of missiles and missile technology."

Many Chinese say they view the U.S. quest for a missile shield as part of a broader strategy of trying to "contain" China and prevent its emergence as a regional power.

"It's very dangerous for the relationship," said Yang Mingjie, director of the arms control and security studies division at the China Institute of Contemporary International Relations, the Chinese Cabinet's think tank.

Already, the perceived threat posed by a U.S. missile shield has spawned a "massive popular sentiment of nationalism" in China, said David Kelly, a senior political lecturer at the Australian

Defense Force Academy in Canberra who is currently doing research in Beijing. "Younger people seem to be more affected by it."

Mr. Bush and other administration officials say they are willing to discuss the concerns of China and other countries, including many U.S. allies. Chinese officials, too, say they are ready to sit down with the United States to exchange ideas on the subject.

But there seems to be little, if any, common ground: Mr. Bush says the U.S. commitment to build a missile-defense system is not negotiable, and Chinese officials say their opposition is also set in stone.

The Bush administration's tougher line toward China—symbolized by the missile-defense plans, some Chinese say—is based on the faulty premise that Beijing is seeking to displace U.S. dominance in Asia and the world, Chinese officials and scholars say.

"The Chinese have really come to value Sino-American relations, and how important the United States is to China's economic development, domestic stability and opening to the outside world," said Dr. Zhu. "From the Chinese point of view, there is no intention of trying to challenge the United States or even balance the States. "

But, at the same time, he said, "the Chinese people feel the United States has been so provocative toward China."

Intentional Arms Race?

One theory, embraced by some in China and the United States, holds that proponents of the American plan are hoping to draw China into an arms race that will drain its resources—a U.S. strategy credited with playing a significant, if not pivotal, role in the downfall of the Soviet Union, scholars and historians say.

Another theory holds that the United States is motivated by a desire to thwart Chinese aims to re-establish its rule over Taiwan, a democratic island of 23 million people that is armed by the United States. A U.S. missile-defense system in East Asia could effectively neutralize hundreds of Chinese missiles aimed at Taiwan, experts say—a situation that could set in motion a deadly chain of events, Chinese officials warn.

"As for theater missile defense for Taiwan, it would be a blatant violation of China's state sovereignty and China's territorial integrity," said Mr. Sha. "It will certainly embolden pro-independence forces in Taiwan. Then you know what would happen," he said—alluding to China's vow to attack Taiwan should it declare independence. "That's the last thing we want to see."

Regardless of the Bush administration's motivations, Beijing would have no choice but to react to a U.S. missile-defense system, Chinese officials and scholars say.

Already, in the aftermath of the April 1 collision of a U.S. surveillance plane and Chinese fighter jet off China's south coast and the announcement last week of a new U.S. arms sale to Taiwan, Chinese leaders are under public pressure to show they are not backing down in the face of perceived American bullying, said Dr. Zhu.

Exactly how China would respond to a U.S. missile-defense system isn't clear. China would likely develop more advanced nuclear weapons—something it is already believed to be doing—and counter-measures to penetrate the U.S. shield, Chinese experts say.

Counter-measures

Since it's much easier for China to devise ways to penetrate the shield than to build its own defensive system, U.S. scientists are already working on ideas for counter-measures to defeat Chinese counter-measures, said a Beijing-based expert on U.S. defense and security policy who didn't want to be quoted by name.

"So, you see, it's just a continuous spiral," said the expert, a senior research fellow at a leading Beijing think tank that is closely following the missile-defense debate. "I think this will be one of the thorniest issues between China and the United States."

Some Chinese officials and scholars say they are hoping that if international appeals don't persuade the Bush administration to abandon its missile-defense plans, technical obstacles will. If the shield is deployed, they are predicting even stormier days ahead in the relationship.

"Chinese-U.S. relations are really at a crossroads, and I think both sides have to make a choice as to what direction the relationship is heading for," said Dr. Zhu. "If the U.S. forces China into a corner, into a military reaction, then maybe we will have to take all measures to counter the American containment policy. China will suffer more than the United States, because China is much weaker. But who will benefit? No one."

In Jiang's Words: "I Hope the Western World Can Understand China Better"[6]

BY ARTHUR SULZBERGER JR., ET AL.
NEW YORK TIMES, AUGUST 10, 2001

Following are excerpts from an interview with President Jiang Zemin by Arthur Sulzberger Jr., publisher of The New York Times; Joseph Lelyveld, executive editor; Howell Raines, who is to succeed Mr. Lelyveld next month; Thomas L. Friedman, foreign affairs columnist; Erik Eckholm, Beijing bureau chief, and three correspondents, Elisabeth Rosenthal, based in Beijing; Craig S. Smith, based in Shanghai; and Mark Landler, based in Hong Kong. Mr. Jiang spoke in Chinese, and a government interpreter translated his remarks.

Q. We'd like to know your sense of President Bush now. He's had two meetings with President Putin of Russia. Do you feel China is being left out?

A. First of all, let me be frank and straightforward. I don't feel at all a sense of being left out. Although I have not met personally President George W. Bush, I have met many times with his parents, George Bush Sr. and his wife. Recently, when I visited President Putin, he briefed me about his meeting with President Bush, and on July 5 this year President Bush called me and we had a conversation. Although it was not a videophone where I could see his facial expression, from his voice I could feel that he was a president we can do business with.

Most of the conversation was conducted with interpreters but at the end, although I do not speak good English, I tried to say directly in English, "Please send my best regards to your parents." . . .

Q. Are you concerned about anti-Chinese sentiment within the administration and some senior officials who seem to regard China as a military threat?

A. . . . I'd like to quote a poem written by a famous poet called Su Dongpo of the Song Dynasty. "People part and meet, they have sorrow and joy, just like the moon that wanes and waxes." Things

---

have been like this for thousands of years. So the only hope is that people can live long and can enjoy the beauty of the moonlight, although they are thousands of miles apart.

Q. Regarding missile defense, is it a threat to China? You have only 20 or 25 missiles able to hit the United States. If we put a shield up, you're out of business.

A. To be frank, it seems that you know how many missiles we have better than I do. I have to say that I have doubts about whether the figure you give is the correct one or not. But let me be clear about one thing. The purpose of our possession of weapons is not for offensive purposes. They are all for our own defense. So we would keep an appropriate number of weapons to meet our defense needs.

Q. If the United States does go ahead with this system, would China be forced to upgrade its nuclear force in response?

"The purpose of our possession of weapons is not for offensive purposes. They are all for our own defense."

A. I think I already addressed this question. We would increase our defense capability in keeping with the development of the international situation, and we would do this for the sole purpose of self-defense. As to when and how we are going to do this, as the chairman of the central military commission, I cannot tell the details. . . .

Q. You've described Taiwan as the most important issue in Chinese-American relations. Some in Washington call for a stronger military relationship with Taiwan, selling more advanced weapons, and to include Taiwan in a theater missile defense. If the United States and Taiwan go this route, how will China respond?

A. We are opposed to U.S. arms sales to Taiwan. After signing of the Aug. 17 Joint Communiqué [of 1982], the U.S. side pledged to reduce its arms sales to Taiwan, both in quantitative and qualitative terms. But in fact what has happened has been the contrary. Secondly, on the one hand the U.S. side has said Taiwan should not go independent. On the other hand, the U.S. provides support to make Taiwan stronger in order to oppose the mainland. This is utterly wrong. Such practice will not serve the interests of the people of Taiwan and is not conducive to peace in Asia, and it will also harm the U.S.'s own interests. . . .

Q. But if the United States goes ahead with more advanced weapons sales, will it be possible for the United States and China to maintain friendly relations?

A. I can only say that it would be very dangerous. Let me add one more point. I hope the Western world can understand China better. This is not simply an issue that has a bearing on myself. It actually has a bearing on the pride and feelings of the 1.2 billion Chinese people and the tens of millions of Chinese descendants overseas.

They all hope that Taiwan and the mainland can be reunified at an early date. So if this situation does not make a turn for the better, does not head toward such a conclusion, then it will be hard to cope with the emotions and desires of so many people.

Q. Many Taiwan companies are investing in China. Do you think that economic integration is the main trend for the future, and at any point will it make the idea of armed conflict just too expensive for both sides?

A. Our intention is peaceful unification and one country, two systems. This has been our consistent position from the beginning. As you rightly point out, many Taiwan business people make investments on the mainland. The reason is simple—because of the favorable investment climate. And Taiwan business people also find themselves in an advantageous position to make investments here, because they are all Chinese, they speak the same language, share the same customs, traditions. If with the increase of economic interaction people on both sides have a strong desire for reunification, then why would it be necessary to resort to armed conflict? . . . Should the pro-independence Taiwanese or the overseas separatist forces intervene in the question of Taiwan and try to separate Taiwan away from the rest of China, China can never renounce the use of force. . . .

> *"Our intention [toward Taiwan] is peaceful unification and one country, two systems."*

Q. The Dalai Lama has said that he supports the principle of "one country, two systems" for Tibet, but China has not been interested in engaging him in conversation on that subject. Is there anything he could say or do that would make possible his return to Tibet?

A. People assume that there is no channel of communication between the central government and the Dalai Lama. In fact, the exchanges and communications have never stopped. Of course not directly with the Dalai, but we have alternate channels. But despite all these communications, we still failed to reach an agreement.

The Dalai has to make a commitment and recognize that Tibet is an inalienable part of China, Taiwan is an inalienable part of China and that the government of the People's Republic of China is the sovereign government of China. He has to recognize all these points. But so far he has not made the complete commitment. He has only made some statements out of context. So it's impossible to have an agreement.

Eleven years ago, I visited Tibet myself. Sea changes have taken place in Tibet since the Dalai left. More than one million serfs were emancipated, and they now lead a happy life with a happy family. I have also climbed to the top floor of the Potala Palace. At that time, it was in very poor shape. The floor was actually shaking, very weak. So we decided to give it a good renovation. We used one ton of gold and spent one hundred million yuan [$12 million] so that its condition has completely changed.

> *"It is impossible for democracy here to be exactly the same as democracy practiced in the Western world."*

Q. How far do you think political change can go in this country, where do you hope it will be 10 years from now? At any point, do you see an independent press and could you imagine the Communist Party allowing competing parties?

A. It seems that Western correspondents and leaders all believe that China is doing very well in its economic reform but doing nothing in its political reform. This is not correct. Actually, our political reform has been always ongoing. What are the main contents of our political reform? They are to strengthen democracy and to strengthen the rule of law. And we need to strengthen and broaden the channels through which democracy can be practiced, including the role of the media. But there's one thing I have to make very clear. It is impossible for democracy here to be exactly the same as democracy practiced in the Western world, as would be preferred by people in the West.

I remember in 1991 former U.S. President Jimmy Carter visited me, and he was very impressed by the direct elections at the village and township level in China. And he said that now you are doing well with the direct democratic election of the village and township chiefs, why not to upgrade it to have direct election for governor of the province, or even president of the country? My reply to him was that it absolutely will not work, because China has a population of 1.26 billion, and over 100 million people still cannot read and write.

How can we have direct elections? I was elected through indirect elections to be president of this country. I was elected by 3,000 deputies to our National People's Congress. I'm presently a deputy to the National People's Congress from Shanghai.

I believe that our world is one of color and diversity. There should be all kinds of election methods. There should not be only one model, the Western model. I have received many U.S. senators and congressmen in Beijing. They ask me why in China there is only one party, the Communist Party. I tell them that no, we also have eight other democratic parties. And then they ask me which among the eight are opposition parties? I tell them that none of the eight are opposition parties because all of them are participating in the discussion and administration of state affairs. . . .

I am 75 years old now. I lived for three-fourths of the last century, and I can tell you with certainty: should China apply the parliamentary democracy of the Western world, the only result will be that 1.2 billion Chinese people will not have enough food to eat. The result will be great chaos, and should that happen it will not be conducive to world peace and stability. [In English] And so I tell you very friendly and frankly, this is my opinion.

Q. What more changes do you expect to see in China in the next five years?

A. It has been made very clear in our 10th five-year plan. Our G.D.P. will continue to grow at a rate of 7 percent annually. And many large-scale projects will be undertaken, and we'll further develop high tech.

Of course, there's no denying that we face a political challenge. For instance, people can be laid off and wait for re-employment. Things like this were unimaginable in the past.

But now people have accepted it as a normal situation, because to improve the efficiency of an enterprise it has to keep the size of the work force at a reasonable level. Therefore, some will be asked to leave their posts and seek re-employment. And over these years, we have developed the social insurance and Social Security system, and we've also extended more job opportunities. . . .

The Chinese people have improved their living standards immensely since the beginning of reform and opening 20 years ago. We should not just envisage where China will find itself in five years' time, we should look into the next 50 years. After 50 years, China will become a country of medium-level development.

Q. Do you think the next generation coming up has any different values and ideas than your generation? If you are asked, will you consider retaining an important position in the government yourself?

A. Undoubtedly the Chinese people are also having these kinds of discussions. Actually I have done a study of the political systems of almost all the developed capitalist countries. I studied the political systems of 27 countries. I moved from Shanghai to work in the central government in 1989, and now more than 12 years have passed. I've seen too much of people being promoted or demoted or retired. But I'm also told that although the leaders change in the Western world, because of the Civil Service the administration will not be affected much.

But according to my observation, once the candidate of a political party gets elected in the Western world, it is quite difficult for him to stay with the program of his predecessor. By the time I leave the historical stage, I don't think there will be any change in the policies, in the direction that we have already set. The next generation of leaders will keep to this road. Maybe I'm too confident.

Q. We are interested in your recent opening of the Communist Party to capitalists and entrepreneurs. Why would you open a workers' party to capitalists?

A. By the time I leave the historical stage, I believe I can be a very good professor in a university, giving lectures about this. Because what we insist on doing is a combination of the fundamental tenets of Marxism applied to the real conditions in China. But we have to know that Marx and Engels lived more than 150 years ago. The *Communist Manifesto* was published 153 years ago. It is impossible to apply every single word or sentence they wrote at that time to today's reality. . . .

Q. Do you surf the Web yourself?

A. My grandson is much more technically proficient than I am. As an electrical engineer, it is not a problem for me to surf on the Net. But I have to admit that it is quite difficult for me to work with the mouse. But people working around me, including my bodyguards, my secretaries and nurses, they all know pretty well now to surf on the Net.

Q. Unfortunately, *The New York Times* Internet site is blocked in this country. We wonder why, and how do you square China's incredible progress with information technology with its practice of

---

"On the question of Chinese entry to W.T.O., I think it will do more good than bad for China's competitiveness in international markets in the 21st century."

---

blocking some important information sources on the Web, such as our newspaper's own Web site?

A. Actually, the answer to this question can be related to my earlier comments. We have a population of 1.2 billion, and stability is very important for them and for them to lead happy lives. Everything has two aspects, pros and cons. The pros of the Internet are that it makes it very easy for people to communicate, to share advances, expertise and information about science and technology. But that aspect is affected by some unhealthy things. You raised a very specific issue about *The New York Times* Web site in particular, I cannot answer this question. But if you ask my view of *The New York Times*, my answer is it is a very good paper. . . .

Q. Does the Internet make it harder for you to rule? Do you hear more from the people now? Is that a big problem for you?

A. It has not caused any inconvenience in administration. As for views from the public, apart from press reports, I also have my own direct channels to know how they feel. I have many, many private friends, like a worker who many years ago, perhaps 40 years ago, was working with me. He talks to me not by e-mail, but by telephone. And professors, and engineers, people from many professions are my friends.

Q. To what extent is joining the W.T.O. a challenge for you, especially managing the social strains that will follow?

A. Everything has two aspects. But on the question of Chinese entry to W.T.O., I think it will do more good than bad for China's competitiveness in international markets in the 21st century. Certain backward industries in China would very much like to have more protection from competition. I told them no. It's just like swimming at Beidaihe. You have to be brave enough to go to the sea. [In English] You have to swim upstream!

Q. What hopes do you have for development of Sino-U.S. relations in the next several years? What helpful steps could President Bush take before his visit in October?

A. It now looks like the momentum is good for bilateral relations. Both sides share a positive desire to have a good relationship. It is in the interest of the whole world. It is in the interest of Asia. It is also in the interest of China and the United States. Not long ago I received visit from Secretary Powell, and President Bush and I talked on the phone.

In October, there will be the APEC meeting in Shanghai, and President Bush will also visit Beijing. All these steps will push the relationship forward.

Q. It sounds like you have a lot on your plate and you just don't want trouble with the U.S. right now. Is that a fair assessment?

A. I think this should be the desire of both countries, not just myself. Let me quote another Chinese proverb—we have too many proverbs in China. "It takes two hands to clap." So it actually depends on the shared desires of both sides.

V. China's Relations with Other States

Editor's Introduction

The articles in this section discuss China's evolving yet frequently thorny relationship with several states, including many of its neighbors. In his article for the *Chicago Tribune*, Michael A. Lev sums up China's relations with Taiwan as follows: "They hate each other but cannot keep apart." China is determined to bring Taiwan, which it views as a renegade province, rather than a separate, sovereign nation, into line, while Taiwan has publicly maintained its political independence. Despite their adversarial relationship, Taiwan has encouraged its companies to invest in China. Both China and Taiwan agree that increased integration benefits both sides economically, though they differ on how it affects their political relationship. According to Lev, China hopes that increased economic integration will eventually bring Taiwan under its control. By contrast, Taiwan has responded to growing economic integration by developing a distinct political identity in order to maintain its independence from China.

One state that is eager to establish diplomatic relations with China is the Vatican, as explained in an article in the *Catholic World Report*. Thus far, the Chinese government has rebuffed Pope John Paul II's overtures until the Vatican meets two demands. First, China wants the Vatican to sever its ties with Taiwan. Second, the Vatican must pledge not to interfere with China's internal affairs, which means that the Pope cannot appoint Catholic bishops in China. This article speculates as to the likelihood that John Paul II would agree to these demands and discusses the pontiff's hope that China will reconsider its stance and establish relations with the Holy See.

Although tensions between China and the Soviet Union once nearly escalated into war, today China and Russia have a more amicable relationship, despite strains which have developed since September 11, 2001. In an article from the *Washington Times*, Nicholas Kralev describes the friendship treaty signed in June 2001 by President Jiang Zemin and Russian President Vladimir Putin, in which both nations pledged to resolve disputes peacefully and work together to promote trade and human rights. Most significantly, Jiang and Putin reaffirmed their support for the 1972 Anti-Ballistic Missile (ABM) Treaty, which they see as a source of international stability. Kralev writes that by reaffirming their support for the ABM Treaty, China and Russia were expressing their opposition to President Bush's plan to deploy a missile defense shield, which critics charge violates the treaty.

The following article discusses the potential effects on China should the current dispute over the Kashmir region escalate into nuclear war between India and Pakistan. Although China has clashed with its close neighbor India in the past and has sold arms to Pakistan, as Frank Langfitt observes in the *Baltimore Sun*, China has adapted its policy toward the two countries in recent years. Today, China takes a neutral stance between them and has urged both countries to settle their disputes peacefully. China's relationship with India has also improved to the point where trade between the two countries tripled from 1995 to 2000.

The next article in this section examines China's relationship with its historical adversary, Japan. According to Robert Marquand in the *Christian Science Monitor*, memories of the Sino-Japanese War during the 1930s and the brutal Japanese occupation of China which followed still divide the two nations. Many Chinese are outraged that several Japanese textbooks minimize and even deny the atrocities committed against Chinese civilians by Japan. Marquand discusses China's campaign begun in the 1990s to educate people about Japan's savage occupation of the country, which lasted until the end of World War II, and the response to this campaign by the international community.

Finally, in the London *Financial Times*, Harvey Morris reports that Israel has been selling weapons and advanced technology to China for over 20 years, a fact that has concerned the U.S. government for some time. In 2000 Israel halted plans to sell advanced technology to China after protests by members of the U.S. Congress, who threatened to cut off military aid to Israel if the sale went forward. The United States fears that China could use Israeli-made technology in a war against Taiwan and sell it to rogue states, such as Iran and Iraq.

China, Taiwan Dance a Mysterious Tango[1]

By Michael A. Lev
CHICAGO TRIBUNE, MARCH 31, 2002

In the past few months, the emotionally charged relationship between China and Taiwan has undergone a quiet upheaval that can be summed up this way: They hate each other but cannot keep apart.

There have been sharp words, petty acts of retribution and gentle wooing by Beijing, but what is more noticeable is Taiwan's seemingly contradictory behavior. It is linking its economy ever closer to China's while simultaneously making a daring political break. The trends are clear, but the meaning behind them is obscured by the extraordinary political sensitivities both sides feel. No one can say for certain whether China and Taiwan are drifting slowly into each other's arms or toward a military showdown.

"You ask if we are at a moment of opportunity or potential crisis, and the answer, somewhat unhelpfully, is both," said Joseph Fewsmith, a China scholar at Boston University.

What Taiwan is doing to generate such confusion is deepening its commitment to investment in China while thumbing its nose at Beijing's leadership.

Easing High-tech Rules

Taiwanese companies are plowing more money than ever before into mainland factories, with the encouragement of Taipei's government, which is relaxing restrictions on high-tech investment and permitting Taiwanese banks to open representative offices in China to serve clients.

Within days, Taiwan's government is expected to announce the next modification of its rules for Chinese investment: It will allow Taiwanese companies to manufacture all but the latest-generation computer chips in mainland factories.

The move follows years of engagement that have led to an investment by Taiwan of more than $50 billion in the economy of its political archrival.

Taiwan has become so dependent on China as a factory floor and marketplace that one analyst said recently that "Taiwan is turning into an economic province of China."

---

1. Article by Michael A. Lev from *Chicago Tribune* March 31, 2002. Copyright © *Chicago Tribune*. Reprinted with permission.

That is the kind of statement that makes Chinese government officials hopeful and Taiwanese officials nervous.

The two sides separated after the communist victory in the 1949 civil war, but Beijing maintains that Taiwan still belongs to China and eventually must return to the fold or face invasion. Taiwan, having developed separately into a democratic, free-market state, has rebuffed China's threats, with U.S. support.

Taiwan has always stepped cautiously, but in recent months it has made several symbolic moves that have broken with tradition and defied Beijing.

The government changed the look of its passports, adding the phrase "issued in Taiwan" to the formal name "Republic of China," thus playing up the image that Taiwan is a separate state rather than an estranged holdover from mainland China's pre-communist days.

It also has flaunted its military relationship with the United States, to China's great annoyance. A Taiwanese defense minister broke precedent in March by visiting the United States, where he attended a conference in Florida and met unofficially with American officials.

In recent months [Taiwan] has made several symbolic moves that have broken with tradition and defied Beijing.

Underpinning of Symbolism

Those kinds of changes may seem innocuous, but the three-way relationship among China, Taiwan and the U.S. is built on carefully balanced symbols. The United States does not have diplomatic relations with Taiwan. It recognizes Beijing as China's government, but it has a legal obligation to sell Taiwan defensive weapons.

China has reacted furiously to the Florida trip, calling in the U.S. ambassador twice for upbraidings and canceling a port call by a U.S. Navy ship at Hong Kong in apparent retaliation.

Beijing believes the U.S. embrace of a Taiwanese official represents a violation of American promises to recognize Beijing's "one China" policy. China said Thursday that it felt "betrayed" and warned that "we are on the verge of another setback in Sino-U.S. relations."

Beijing mistrusts Taiwan's president, Chen Shui-bian, whose political party supports independence. And it worries that Taiwan—benefiting from White House support—is slowly pulling away from China.

But at the same time that China is warning of a "freezing wind" in relations with the U.S. over Taiwan, Beijing is engaged in a goodwill campaign that may turn out to be as significant as any other development.

Bow to Taiwan Government

In a recent speech that has been analyzed endlessly by China experts, Chinese Deputy Prime Minister Qian Qichen appeared to offer the first step in recognizing Taiwan's recent political development.

He said members of President Chen's political party would be welcome to visit China. It was another modest-sounding symbol, but one that carried an important message: Beijing was ready to acknowledge that Taiwan was governed by a political party that favors independence.

There is more than one way to analyze all the pulling and tugging between Taiwan and China, and whether it adds up to a relationship that is warming or stiffening.

Taiwanese officials say it is wrong to connect too many of the dots. Taiwan is pursuing economic opportunities in China while exploring its separate political identity, without rejecting the idea of negotiating with Beijing. Its one condition is that Taiwan must be recognized as an equal, not a subject. China rejects that idea.

Taiwanese officials say no more than 20 percent of the economy is dependent on China. What links its economic and political initia-

> *Taiwanese officials say no more than 20 percent of the economy is dependent on China.*

tives is the idea that business ties will promote understanding and lead to a discussion of political integration.

"Maybe it will take a long time—20, 30 years—but I think it's a reasonable and peaceful way to go," said Chen Ming-Tong of Taiwan's Mainland Affairs Council.

Some Beijing watchers feel China is softening its approach to Taiwan because it is beginning to panic that the island will continue to drift away unless the door opens soon to negotiations. Others believe China has calculated that the deepening of economic ties will tip the balance in Beijing's favor.

That is the fear that grips many in Taiwan, and it explains why some do not want more of the island's high-tech industry to migrate to the mainland.

Taiwan maintains some restrictions on investment and has rejected Chinese offers to open direct air, sea and postal links between the two sides. Today, all transportation and investment links are indirect, mainly through Hong Kong.

Avoiding a "Black Hole"

Taiwanese analysts say the fear of being swallowed up by China is one of the main reasons Taiwan has been so eager to promote its own political identity: as protection.

"A lot of people think China is a black hole," said Philip Yang, a political scientist at National Taiwan University. "They worry that with further integration we'll lose our identity and breathing space in international affairs, and that's the reason they hope to increase creeping diplomacy.

"We're worried about this question of whether time is on our side. China thinks it's inevitable that Taiwan will have to accept their formula because they have the upper hand in terms of cross-Strait integration."

The reverse argument also exists: that China is too wrapped up in its own problems to worry about the island, giving Taipei an opening to explore its political identity while riding China's economic coattails.

What analysts all hope for is that whatever the pace of change, no one miscalculates, leading to a confrontation that could drag all three sides toward war.

Pope Seeks to Pursue Diplomatic Ties

But Beijing Shows No Interest[2]

CATHOLIC WORLD REPORT, DECEMBER 2001

Pope John Paul II has called upon the Chinese government to resume negotiations toward the establishment of normal diplomatic relations.

The Pope's message was contained in a 4-page letter—made available in Chinese and English as well as Italian—published in conjunction with a Gregorian University conference on the missionary work of Matteo Ricci. Rumors had circulated in Rome, earlier in the autumn, that the conference—which opened on October 24—would be the occasion for the announcement of diplomatic relations between the Holy See and Beijing. Those rumors were proven false by the Holy Father's plea to the Chinese government. The Pontiff made it clear that talks with Beijing had broken down.

After praising the work of Father Matteo Ricci—the 16th-century missionary—the Pope said that today, too, it is important to promote friendship and dialogue between "the two oldest living institutions in the world," the Catholic Church and the Chinese government. He added that the "opening of some space for dialogue" between the two parties would constitute "an improvement for all humanity."

Asking pardon for any errors committed by Catholics in the past, the Pope said that today, "The Catholic Church is not asking for any privilege from China or from her political authorities, but only the chance to engage in dialogue, to work toward a relationship marked by mutual respect and deeper understanding."

Following up on the papal statement, one ranking Vatican official said that the Pontiff is anxious to sign an accord with the government of China, and would bend diplomatic protocol if necessary in order to break a 50-year diplomatic stalemate. Archbishop Giuseppe Pittau, the secretary of the Congregation for Catholic Education, told the Italian daily newspaper *Avvenire* that the Pope "would be ready to sign an accord with China tomorrow." The Jesuit prelate said that the Pontiff is frustrated by a situation which is "frozen in place," and would immediately accept an invitation to visit Beijing.

---

2. Article from *Catholic World Report* December 2001. Copyright © *Catholic World Report*. Reprinted with permission.

As for the two conditions that Beijing has consistently stipulated as the basis for any discussion of diplomatic relations—a Vatican promise not to interfere in "internal affairs" (including the naming of Catholic bishops), and a break in diplomatic relations between the Holy See and Taiwan—Archbishop Pittau expressed confidence that "technical solutions" could be found to allow an agreement.

Taiwan's ambassador to the Holy See immediately expressed doubts that the government of China would respond favorably to the Pope's appeal. Raymond Tai said that the Holy Father's overture to Beijing was "exceptional," but that the Chinese government would not respond in kind. The Taiwanese ambassador offered these opinions after having had lunch with Msgr. Celestino Migliore, the Vatican's under-secretary of state. The envoy met with the Vatican official on the day after the Pope's public appeal—obviously hoping to clarify the diplomatic situation.

Ambassador Tai reported that he had been assured that the Holy See was not expecting any immediate response from Beijing. The Taiwanese diplomat also noted that the Chinese government has rebuffed every previous effort to establish diplomatic ties with Rome, and "the conditions are always the same." Beijing has always

> *The Chinese government has rebuffed every previous effort to establish diplomatic ties with Rome, and "the conditions are always the same."*

demanded that the Communist Party, rather than the Vatican, should approve Catholic bishops. Also, the Chinese government has insisted that the Holy See must break off diplomatic relations with Taiwan.

In fact, the Holy See does not have a diplomatic mission to Taiwan itself. The Vatican embassy in China was originally stationed in Beijing, but moved first to Nanking, then Hong Kong, and finally to Taiwan in order to avoid the onslaught of the Communist regime. The Vatican's nuncio in Taiwan remains, for official purposes, the Pope's legate to all of China.

Ambassador Tai told the Roman news agency I Media that, in his view, the canonization of 120 Chinese martyrs last October was a bitter pill for the Chinese Communist leadership, and had the effect of erecting a "higher barrier" to diplomatic accords. Although the Vatican insisted at the time that there was "no political or diplomatic consideration" involved in the canonizations—that the ceremony had been timed to match the celebration of missionary work during the Jubilee year—Communist leaders were furious to note that the canonizations took place on the anniversary of the establishment of the People's Republic in China.

Beijing had opposed the canonizations, saying that the missionaries represented an "imperialistic" influence on China. The Communist government has been engaged in a long tug-of-war for the affections of Chinese Catholics, insisting that "patriotic" Catholics must sever their connections with the "foreign" influence of the Holy See.

While the Taiwanese envoy was happy to discuss the implications of the Pope's dramatic gesture, the Communist Party leadership in Beijing was not at all anxious to respond. After several days of silence, the Chinese Foreign Ministry issued a bland statement saying that the government would study the Pope's statement. The Foreign Ministry added, however, that China would not bend on its two familiar demands: that the Holy See sever relations with Taiwan and promise not to interfere in China's "internal" religious affairs.

Russia, China Ink Friendship Pact in Moscow[3]

By Nicholas Kralev
Washington Times, July 17, 2001

The leaders of Russia and China yesterday signed their first friendship treaty in 50 years and reaffirmed support for the ABM Treaty to curb U.S. missile-defense plans.

The treaty, signed yesterday by Russian President Vladimir Putin and Chinese President Jiang Zemin, affirmed the strategic friendship and cooperation between Moscow and Beijing, bitter rivals for influence in the communist world during the Cold War.

"We believe that more active cooperation between our countries in discussing missile defenses and disarmament will enhance our efforts in building a multipolar world and establishing a fair, rational international order," Mr. Jiang said, referring to the dominant role of the United States in global affairs.

Calling the document "historic," Mr. Putin, said: " . . . we presume this document will form the basis for stability in international relations as a whole." The treaty, which replaces an outdated 1950 version signed by Josef Stalin and Mao Tse-tung that failed to prevent a 1969 border war, commits the signatories to "mutual efforts to support global strategic balance and stability."

The United States yesterday downplayed the effect of a new treaty on Washington's global role and said it didn't see the pact as "any particular threat to us or to our plans."

Reiterating U.S. determination to go ahead with its plans, the State Department said the Russia-China pact would not change the strategic balance of power, because it was not a defense alliance between the two countries.

"We've never felt that this was a zero-sum game," said Richard Boucher, State Department spokesman. "We've felt that it's important for us to have good relations with Russia and with China, and we've always felt it's important for them to have good relations with each other. They have a long border in a key region, and it's important for them to get along. So we don't see it as any particular threat to us or to our plans."

Although they said the document was not aimed at a third party, Mr. Putin and Mr. Jiang reaffirmed their faith in the 1972 Anti-Ballistic Missile Treaty (ABM) as the cornerstone of international sta-

---

A Beautiful Friendship?

China and Russia signed an 11-page friendship and cooperation pact in the Kremlin to replace an agreement inked at the beginning of the Cold War. Excerpts from agreements reached between the two:

SECURITY COOPERATION: "The two sides agree not to use force, or threaten to use force, nor to use economic or other forms of pressure against one another, and agree to solve joint disputes exclusively through peaceful means. The two sides confirm their commitment not to use, or aim, nuclear weapons against one another."

CHECHNYA AND TAIWAN: "The Chinese side supports the policies of Russia on questions concerning its defense of the national unity and territorial integrity of the Russian Federation. . . . The Russian side speaks out against the independence of Taiwan in any form."

BORDER DISPUTES: "The two signatories agree to continue negotiations to resolve questions concerning the disputed portions of the Sino-Russian border."

TRADE: "The two sides, on the basis of mutual benefit, are developing cooperation in the spheres of trade and the economy, military-technological cooperation, science, energy and transportation, nuclear energy" and others areas.

HUMAN RIGHTS: "The two sides are cooperating in the sphere of human rights and basic freedoms in accordance with their own international obligations and the national laws that apply in the two countries."

EXTERNAL RELATIONS: "This agreement does not affect the rights of the two countries in relation to other international agreements, and is not aimed against any third state."

MISSILE DEFENSE: The two countries "underline the principal importance of the 1972 Anti-Ballistic Missile Treaty, which remains the cornerstone of strategic stability and the basis for reducing strategic arms forces, and reaffirm their support of the treaty in its current form."

Source: Agence France-Presse

---

bility. The Bush administration has said the treaty, which is the only hurdle to building a missile-defense shield, should be scrapped or substantially amended.

In Moscow, where Mr. Jiang is on a four-day visit, the two leaders said the Good Neighborly Treaty of Friendship and Cooperation would help safeguard peace.

The Russia-China summit followed a successful test of the U.S. anti-missile system, which was condemned in both capitals, as well as Beijing's victory in the bid for hosting the 2008 summer Olympic Games on Friday. Mr. Putin flies to Genoa, Italy, later this week for the annual gathering of the world's leading economies and Russia, where missile defense is certain to be high on the agenda.

Both Moscow and Beijing denounced the U.S. missile test, with Russia asking, "why should we lead things to a point where we threaten the whole architecture in the field of nuclear disarmament and nonproliferation, at the heart of which lies" the ABM agreement.

China's Foreign Ministry said, "It is not favorable to global strategic balance and stability."

In the new treaty, Russia reiterated its support for the Chinese claim on Taiwan, which Beijing views as a renegade province.

"Russia acknowledges that there is only one China, the government of the People's Republic of China is the only legitimate government representing all of China, and Taiwan is an inalienable part of China," the document said. "Russia opposes any kind of independence for Taiwan."

Mr. Putin and Mr. Jiang also pledged to resolve two small remaining border disputes and to boost trade. Although China has bought billions of dollars worth of Russian jets, submarines, missiles and destroyers, Moscow's trade with Beijing is still far short of China's annual trade with Japan or the United States.

"We have a realistic view of the situation," Mr. Putin said. "Russia accounts for just 2 percent in China's trade, but that means that we have good prospects."

The two leaders agreed to expand cooperation in the spheres of oil and gas, energy, aircraft building, communications and new technologies.

In Washington, a report issued yesterday by the East-West Institute's Bipartisan Task Force pronounced a "historic opportunity" to redefine the nature of U.S.-Russian relations.

Former Sen. Alan K. Simpson, co-chairman of the task force, told reporters and editors at *The Washington Times* that "the time has come to listen and not to lecture" the Russian people.

The report makes a number of recommendations, including increased transparency on the part of both countries, discussion of the security relationship and U.S. promotion of "Russia's integration into global institutions such as the World Trade Organization."

Although "transparency is an overused word, it's critical that we both know what we're doing," Mr. Simpson said.

China's Leader Visits India to Urge Peace without Taking Sides[4]

BY FRANK LANGFITT
BALTIMORE SUN, JANUARY 13, 2002

When India's ambassador to China arrived for a dinner at the Great Hall of the People here in the early 1970s, Chinese officials served his food early because they knew he wouldn't be staying long.

The two countries were bitter rivals. China strongly backed India's archenemy, Pakistan, and endorsed Pakistan's call for self-determination in Kashmir, the disputed Himalayan region over which India and Pakistan had fought two wars. During the dinner, Chinese officials spoke out on the Kashmir issue, and India's ambassador walked out in protest. When Chinese Premier Zhu Rongji arrives in New Delhi today for a six-day visit, he won't be taking sides on Kashmir, the region that has once again brought India and Pakistan to the brink of war. Instead, Chinese officials say, Zhu will remain neutral and urge that India and Pakistan try to negotiate a solution.

Zhu's visit and its tone demonstrate how China's policy toward South Asia has evolved since the end of the Cold War. After decades of arming and supporting Pakistan as a proxy against India, China has developed a more balanced and independent relationship with South Asia's archrivals.

The trip, which was planned long before the current tensions in Kashmir, also provides China with a chance to flex its diplomatic muscles after sitting on the sidelines of the Afghan war.

In recent years, China had organized an anti-terrorism group with Russia and six Central Asian states. Since the terrorist attacks of Sept. 11, Beijing has offered verbal support for a global war against terrorism but played only a marginal role.

Economic Considerations

In addition to visiting New Delhi, Zhu will travel to Bombay and Bangalore, where the Chinese hope to learn from India's booming software export industry. The premier's trip is designed to build on steadily improving relations with India and to expand economic ties between the two Asian giants.

---

4. Article by Frank Langfitt, *Baltimore Sun* January 13, 2002. Copyright © *Baltimore Sun*. Reprinted with permission.

From 1995 to 2000, China's trade with India nearly tripled, to $2.9 billion from $1.1 billion. Contact between the nations is still so limited, though, that no direct flights between their capitals exist.

"It's high time for the Chinese premier to pay this visit," said Cheng Ruisheng, who served as China's ambassador to India from 1991 to 1994. "There has been some kind of mistrust in the mind of the Indian government and the mind of the Indian people. To increase these mutual exchanges at the highest level is very important for both countries."

The last Chinese premier to travel to India was Li Peng, who visited in 1991.

For much of the past half-century, Sino-Indian relations have been marked by distrust and rivalry. Some of the tensions have arisen from the countries' similarities, others from differences.

India and China have developing economies and huge populations. They are also ambitious nuclear powers that yearn for international respect.

For much of the past half-century, Sino-Indian relations have been marked by distrust and rivalry.

The two nations share a 2,500-mile border over which they fought a brief, bloody war in 1962.

China claimed that India conducted nuclear tests in 1998 as part of a drive to be recognized as a global power and to gain a permanent seat on the United Nations Security Council. The tests drew international condemnation and inspired Pakistan to follow with tests of its own.

India said it conducted the nuclear tests because of China, noting a threat from Beijing's nuclear arsenal, its tradition of military support for Pakistan and the nations' unresolved border dispute.

India and China are very different political states. India is the world's largest democracy, though a messy and often inefficient one. China operates under a sometimes brutal, authoritarian system and is home to the last major Communist Party on the planet.

New Delhi's and Beijing's political differences have led to tensions over Tibet. India has served as home for the Tibetan government-in-exile since the Dalai Lama fled there in 1959 after a failed uprising against Chinese rule.

India recognizes Tibet as an autonomous region of China, but provides sanctuary for Tibetan refugees.

One of Tibetan Buddhism's most important figures, the 16-year-old Karmapa Lama, fled from China across the Himalayas in 2000 to northern India, where the Dalai Lama welcomed him. The episode embarrassed China, which has tried to co-opt and control Tibetan religious leaders and portrays its rule there as benevolent.

India handled the case gingerly. Last year, New Delhi quietly granted the boy refugee status.

"Although the Indian government says it does not support the Dalai Lama . . . there are different opinions towards the Tibet issue within India," said Shang Huipeng, an Indian specialist at Beijing University. "They (Chinese leaders) don't trust India."

Of the two countries, China has proved by far the better economic performer over the past two decades. Its market reforms have led to higher growth rates, standards of living and levels of foreign investment.

Although the two nations have similar-sized populations—China has 1.3 billion people; India has about 1 billion—China's economy is nearly three times as large.

China and India enjoyed a period of warm relations in the 1950s when the countries were led by Mao Tse-tung and Jawaharlal Nehru, who espoused a vision of Asian brotherhood. That dream ended in 1962 when China seized a large swath of the Himalayas claimed by India. China won a brief war, and 40,000 Indian soldiers died, setting the stage for a rivalry that continues today.

After the fighting, China pursued close relations with Pakistan, India's enemy since their violent partition at the time they gained independence from Britain in 1947. Beijing provided nuclear weapon designs to Islamabad as well as weapons material. U.S. intelligence officials believe China also sold nuclear-capable M-11 missiles to Pakistan in 1992.

Shift toward Neutral Position

By then, though, Beijing had begun to improve ties with India. China reconsidered their antagonistic relationship in the 1980s. The change arose in part from China's desire to maintain peace on its borders so it could develop its economy without distractions.

The shift also acknowledges political reality: India's military is stronger than Pakistan's, and its population and economy are many times larger, making it South Asia's dominant power.

In the 1990s, New Delhi and Beijing pledged not to use force to resolve their continuing border dispute, but still jockey for position.

Despite its rapprochement with New Delhi, Beijing has not forgotten Pakistan.

Pakistan's president, Gen. Pervez Musharraf, has traveled to the Chinese capital twice in recent weeks. The first visit included a meeting with Chinese President Jiang Zemin and marked a half-century of Sino-Pakistani relations. The second was billed as a refueling stop on the way to a regional summit in Katmandu, Tibet.

Why the Past Still Separates China and Japan[5]

By Robert Marquand
Christian Science Monitor, August 20, 2001

When Sun Chuan Ben fixed roofs at a Japanese base in the waning days of World War II, he was told not to ask questions. But he wondered why so many buildings were stacked with cages of yellow rats.

Only later did he, and other Chinese, begin to learn what went on at Unit 731, a huge complex in northeast China. As both Chinese and surviving Japanese soldiers now allege, most recently in testimony before a Tokyo court, between 1938 and 1945 the germ-warfare research unit conducted experiments on Chinese people and worked on methods to spread disease, using animals from rats to camels. Japan has never officially acknowledged any wrongdoing at Unit 731.

That is one reason why, when Japanese Prime Minister Junichiro Koizumi paid homage to Japan's war dead at a shrine last week, and when Japan's Education Ministry this summer approved history textbooks that whitewash or deny mass crimes by Japanese troops in Korea and China—those acts echo loudly in Asia in a way that is unpredictable, largely negative, and easily exploitable by right-wing factions.

"I am not against the Japanese people, I do not hate them," says Mr. Sun. "But I will not be friends with those Japanese who wish to deny what happened."

Such vocal disagreements also symbolize why, while Japan is China's top trading partner—ahead of the U.S.—the China-Japan relationship remains the thickest and most complex Gordian Knot in Pacific relations.

These latest echoes also illustrate the complex psychological legacy of the war in Asia—something never reconciled in this part of the world, or examined in the way that Nazi crimes in Europe have been over time. Experts say it's a main reason why the security and diplomatic relationships that took hold in Europe after World War II have not taken place in this part of the world.

"As the 21st century begins, Asia's security environment seems likely to be shaped by the distrust, if not rivalry, between China and Japan that is the legacy of the past century," says Richard Solomon, director of the U.S. Institute of Peace in Washington and a former China specialist at the U.S. State Department.

The Unit 731 museum—which opened in June with 12 rooms of exhibits of rusty equipment, gas masks, photo documentaries, and acres of preserved ruins—is just one of many highly produced permanent exhibitions built in China during the 1990's, under an official campaign to highlight and educate about "the Anti-Japanese War of Aggression," the term given to Japan's 13-year occupation of China.

"When we see Koizumi walk to the shrine, we want to invite him to come here," says Wang Peng, manager of the exhibit. "The Japanese deny this germ-warfare center ever existed."

Koizumi, in his statement at the Yakasuni shrine last week, offered "profound remorse . . . to all the victims of the war" and said due to a "mistaken policy . . . Japan imposed . . . immeasurable ravages and suffering . . . to the people of . . . Asia."

Precise knowledge about Unit 731 is sketchy by Western standards. The Japanese blew up the laboratories before they left, and China spent four more years in a civil war that brought in Communist rule. Most of the substantial evidence about the complex has come from former Japanese workers who broke their silence late in life.

One such worker, Yoshio Shinozuka, testified last year that he cultivated fleas that were exposed to rats with bubonic plague. Other accounts compiled in recent years suggest that Chinese prisoners were subjected to bubonic plague, frostbite, extreme heat, toxic gas, amputation, vivisection, and electric shocks. Some 3,000 people are estimated to have died inside the complex—though Chinese officials say the number is higher.

More deeply in the Chinese mind, say some local scholars, is a sense that by never fully apologizing, and by minimizing wartime atrocities, the Japanese are subtly jabbing at the Chinese—implying cultural superiority by suggesting that it was not China, but the United States, that defeated Japan in 1945. "It is a way for Japanese to tell us we are inferior," says one retired scholar.

Japanese sources say Tokyo has apologized on three separate occasions, and that the Chinese are continuing to use the war as a "history card" to gain leverage and sympathy internationally. "The Chinese keep banging us, beating us. What do they want? They teach young people that Japanese are untrustworthy, and beasts," says one well-placed Japanese official. "We don't teach our children they are beasts."

Some China scholars say the Chinese Communist Party also uses the war as a way to legitimize itself through a patriotic appeal. Some point out that while Beijing has sought to highlight Japanese aggression in World War II, it is woefully lacking in coming to terms with its own history—events like the Great Famine of the late 1950s, in which millions died, the Cultural Revolution, and the more recent Tiananmen Square episode of 1989.

One diplomat speculates that the war is kept alive in China partly because the Chinese Communists were never able to confront the Japanese military directly after the war. The government-in-exile of Chiang Kai Shek represented China at the 1951 San Francisco Peace Treaty.

In 1972, the Japanese sought quickly to establish relations with China after U.S. President Nixon cleared the way, which led to a rapprochement without much historical reconciliation. Under a 1978 peace treaty, China gave up its right to claim reparations from the Japanese government, in the view of some experts. "In the heart of the Communist army, there was never a chance to say 'We won,'" says the diplomat. "They have not lost that obsession."

Yet Chinese say the main reason the war is kept alive is due to what they regard as Japan's two decade-long campaign to deny wartime atrocities. Cases such as Unit 731 pale in comparison with the Japanese massacre at Nanjing between December 1937 and May, 1938—when an estimated 300,000 Chinese died. Japanese textbooks never treated the Nanjing event in anything but a cursory manner, and Tokyo has never taken responsibility.

"Not until 1994 were Japanese schoolchildren taught that [Emperor] Hirohito's army was responsible for the deaths of at least 20 million Allied soldiers and Asian civilians during World War II," writes author Iris Chang in *The Rape of Nanjing*, a 1996 account of Japanese brutality and the contemporary effort by Tokyo to sanitize its past.

"When the Japanese came out with a textbook that denied the Nanjing massacre and lied about the Japanese invasion, when they started to build monuments to their troops, that hurt us—and we realized it was time to do something," says Han Xiao, an official with the Unit 731 exhibit. "We want these museums to tell the truth to all peoples of the world, and especially to educate the younger generations, so it won't happen again."

Younger generations of Chinese, however, have developed very independent views of Japan. One student interviewed said "we should not forget," as one put it. But many also look to Tokyo for the latest music and fashions. At an exhibition of Japanese student art in Harbin, one student says, "Let the past be the past. I think it was natural for Koizumi to visit the shrine."

Israel's Arms Ties with China Haunting U.S.[6]

By Harvey Morris
Financial Times, March 21, 2001

One sensitive issue hovering in the background of Ariel Sharon's first visit to Washington as Israeli prime minister is that of his country's controversial arms relationship with China.

Israel's most recent planned sale of high-tech weaponry to Beijing was the cause of a rare public spat with the U.S. during the premiership of Ehud Barak, Mr Sharon's predecessor.

The dispute last year involved Israel's contract to supply Beijing with the Phalcon airborne early warning radar system developed by Elta, a subsidiary of Israel Aircraft Industries. The deal was frozen after a congressional committee protested, amid threats to cut military aid to Israel, that the sale would give China a military edge over Taiwan. Israeli military analysts say that, while Mr Sharon is eager not to revive the dispute, some officials and defence industry executives are smarting over what they regard as U.S. interference in Israel's affairs and still hope the sale will go ahead.

"The project was frozen but not killed," said Gerald Steinberg, a Middle East arms expert at Israel's Bar-Ilan University. "Some people in the military industries lobby think they can still salvage it."

He said there had already been relatively low-level discussions with Washington since the Phalcon affair over how to handle such deals. "The U.S. would like to be able to give prior approval and Israel wants to limit that. At the same time Israel wants to avoid another (dispute). Barak handled it very badly and Sharon has learned the lesson."

Meanwhile Phalcon's manufacturers are focusing on selling a scaled-down version of the radar system, an option being discussed with U.S. officials.

Israel is eager to maximise its arms exports, a sector that grew 10 per cent in 2000 to Dollars 2.35bn (Pounds 1.65bn), with Asia the key market. The Phalcon deal with China would have been worth Dollars 1.5bn over several years.

---

6. Article by Harvey Morris from *Financial Times* March 21, 2001. Copyright © *Financial Times*. Reprinted with permission.

The Phalcon affair and the prospect of future sales of the system, which Mr Sharon was not expected to raise during his Washington visit, have focused attention on a secretive weapons relationship with China that dates back 20 years, long before the two countries established diplomatic relations in 1992.

It is a partnership that has long worried the U.S. Congress, whose concerns involve not only Taiwan but also the possibility that China could leak Israeli high-tech weaponry, much of it funded by the U.S. taxpayer, to states such as Iraq and Iran.

Israel itself recognised that risk in 1999, when it raised its concerns that China was transferring missile technology to Iran. Shortly after the Gulf war in 1991, the administration of President George Bush Snr acknowledged it was investigating the possible transfer by Israel of Patriot missile technology to China.

U.S.-built Patriot batteries were set up in Israel amid great fanfare during the war as a defence against Iraqi Scud missile attacks and as a gesture to keep Israel out of the conflict.

A report about the same time by the Rand Corporation described Israel as "China's leading foreign supplier of advanced technology" and, in 1999, the congressional Cox committee reported that Israel had offered significant technology co-operation to China in missile and aircraft, including its F-10 fighter.

U.S. defence journals reported that the F-10 had the same configuration as Israel's Lavi fighter, a project dropped in 1987 after it had been funded by the U.S. to the tune of some Dollars 1.5bn.

The U.S. official principally responsible for killing the Lavi was Dov Zakheim, a defence department analyst, who concluded that the U.S. would have to provide Dollars 16bn in support over the lifetime of the project.

An Orthodox Jew, Mr Zakheim was publicly attacked for appearing to go against the interests of Israel. He maintained that U.S. military aid would be better spent acquiring U.S. fighter technology off the shelf, modernising the Israeli navy or upgrading its ground forces.

His arguments eventually persuaded the Israeli Knesset to halt expenditure on the project in 1992. Mr Zakheim's experience with the Israelis will no doubt come in useful in his new post. Among President Bush's cabinet appointments, Mr Zakheim has been named under-secretary of defence.

Appendix

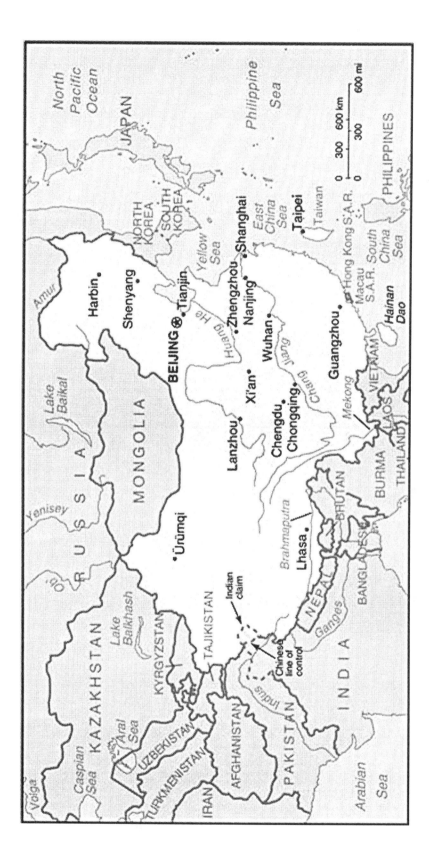

China

From *The World Factbook 2001*, prepared by the Central Intelligence Agency of the United States, *www.cia.gov*.

Introduction

Background: For centuries China has stood as a leading civilization, outpacing the rest of the world in the arts and sciences. But in the first half of the 20th century, China was beset by major famines, civil unrest, military defeats, and foreign occupation. After World War II, the Communists under MAO Zedong established a dictatorship that, while ensuring China's sovereignty, imposed strict controls over everyday life and cost the lives of tens of millions of people. After 1978, his successor DENG Xiaoping gradually introduced market-oriented reforms and decentralized economic decision making. Output quadrupled in the next 20 years and China now has the world's second largest GDP. Political controls remain tight even while economic controls continue to weaken.

Geography

Location: Eastern Asia, bordering the East China Sea, Korea Bay, Yellow Sea, and South China Sea, between North Korea and Vietnam

Geographic coordinates: 35' N, 105' E

Map references: Asia

Area:
  total: 9,596,960 sq km
  land: 9,326,410 sq km
  water: 270,550 sq km

Area—comparative: slightly smaller than the U.S.

Land boundaries:
  total: 22,147.24 km
  border countries: Afghanistan 76 km, Bhutan 470 km, Burma 2,185 km, Hong Kong 30 km, India 3,380 km, Kazakhstan 1,533 km, North Korea 1,416 km, Kyrgyzstan 858 km, Laos 423 km, Macau 0.34 km, Mongolia 4,676.9 km, Nepal 1,236 km, Pakistan 523 km, Russia (northeast) 3,605 km, Russia (northwest) 40 km, Tajikistan 414 km, Vietnam 1,281 km

Coastline: 14,500 km

Maritime claims:
  contiguous zone: 24 NM
  continental shelf: 200 NM or to the edge of the continental margin
  territorial sea: 12 NM

Climate: extremely diverse; tropical in south to subarctic in north

Terrain: mostly mountains, high plateaus, deserts in west; plains, deltas, and hills in east

Elevation extremes:
lowest point: Turpan Pendi—154 m
highest point: Mount Everest 8,850 m (1999 est.)

Natural resources: coal, iron ore, petroleum, natural gas, mercury, tin, tungsten, antimony, manganese, molybdenum, vanadium, magnetite, aluminum, lead, zinc, uranium, hydropower potential (world's largest)

Land use:
arable land: 10%
permanent crops: 0%
permanent pastures: 43%
forests and woodland: 14%
other: 33% (1993 est.)

Irrigated land: 498,720 sq km (1993 est.)

Natural hazards: frequent typhoons (about five per year along southern and eastern coasts); damaging floods; tsunamis; earthquakes; droughts

Environment—current issues: air pollution (greenhouse gases, sulfur dioxide particulates) from reliance on coal, produces acid rain; water shortages, particularly in the north; water pollution from untreated wastes; deforestation; estimated loss of one-fifth of agricultural land since 1949 to soil erosion and economic development; desertification; trade in endangered species

Environment—international agreements:
party to: Antarctic-Environmental Protocol, Antarctic Treaty, Biodiversity, Climate Change, Desertification, Endangered Species, Hazardous Wastes, Law of the Sea, Marine Dumping, Nuclear Test Ban, Ozone Layer Protection, Ship Pollution, Tropical Timber 83, Tropical Timber 94, Wetlands, Whaling
signed, but not ratified: Climate Change–Kyoto Protocol, Marine Life Conservation

Geography—*note*: world's fourth-largest country (after Russia, Canada, and U.S.); Mount Everest on the border with Nepal, is the world's tallest peak

People

Population: 1,273,111,290 (July 2001 est.)

Age structure:
0–14 years: 25.01% (male 166,754,893; female 151,598,117)
15–64 years: 67.88% (male 445,222,858; female 418,959,646)
65 years and over: 7.11% (male 42,547,296; female 48,028,480) (2001 est.)

Population growth rate: 0.88% (2001 est.)

Birth rate: 15.95 births/1,000 population (2001 est.)

Death rate: 6.74 deaths/1,000 population (2001 est.)

Net migration rate: -0.39 migrant(s)/1,000 population (2001 est.)

Sex ratio:
at birth: 1.09 male(s)/female
under 15 years: 1.1 male(s)/female
15–64 years: 1.06 male(s)/female
65 years and over: 0.89 male(s)/female
total population: 1.06 male(s)/female (2001 est.)

Infant mortality rate: 28.08 deaths/1,000 live births (2001 est.)

Life expectancy at birth:
total population: 71.62 years
male: 69.81 years
female: 73.59 years (2001 est.)

Total fertility rate: 1.82 children born/woman (2001 est.)

HIV/AIDS—adult prevalence rate: 0.07% (1999 est.)

HIV/AIDS—people living with HIV/AIDS: 500,000 (1999 est.)

HIV/AIDS—deaths: 17,000 (1999 est.)

Nationality:
noun: Chinese (singular and plural)
adjective: Chinese

Ethnic groups: Han Chinese 91.9%, Zhuang, Uygur, Hui, Yi, Tibetan, Miao, Manchu, Mongol, Buyi, Korean, and other nationalities 8.1%

Religions: Daoist (Taoist), Buddhist, Muslim 2%–3%, Christian 1% (est.)

Note: officially atheist

Languages: Standard Chinese or Mandarin (Putonghua, based on the Beijing dialect), Yue (Cantonese), Wu (Shanghaiese), Minbei (Fuzhou), Minnan (Hokkien-Taiwanese), Xiang, Gan, Hakka dialects, minority languages (see Ethnic groups entry)

Literacy:
definition: age 15 and over can read and write
total population: 81.5%
male: 89.9%
female: 72.7% (1995 est.)

Government

Country name:

conventional long form: People's Republic of China
conventional short form: China
local long form: Zhonghua Renmin Gongheguo
local short form: Zhong Guo
abbreviation: PRC

Government type: Communist state

Capital: Beijing

Administrative divisions: 23 provinces (sheng, singular and plural), 5 autonomous regions* (zizhiqu, singular and plural), and 4 municipalities** (shi, singular and plural); Anhui, Beijing**, Chongqing**, Fujian, Gansu, Guangdong, Guangxi*, Guizhou, Hainan, Hebei, Heilongjiang, Henan, Hubei, Hunan, Jiangsu, Jiangxi, Jilin, Liaoning, Nei Mongol*, Ningxia*, Qinghai, Shaanxi, Shandong, Shanghai**, Shanxi, Sichuan, Tianjin**, Xinjiang*, Xizang* (Tibet), Yunnan, Zhejiang; *note*—China considers Taiwan its 23rd province; see separate entries for the special administrative regions of Hong Kong and Macau

Independence: 221 B.C. (unification under the Qin or Ch'in Dynasty 221 B.C.; Qing or Ch'ing Dynasty replaced by the Republic on 12 February 1912; People's Republic established 1 October 1949)

National holiday: Founding of the People's Republic of China, 1 October (1949)

Constitution: most recent promulgation 4 December 1982

Legal system: a complex amalgam of custom and statute, largely criminal law; rudimentary civil code in effect since 1 January 1987; new legal codes in effect since 1 January 1980; continuing efforts are being made to improve civil, administrative, criminal, and commercial law

Suffrage: 18 years of age; universal

Executive branch:

chief of state: President JIANG Zemin (since 27 March 1993) and Vice President HU Jintao (since 16 March 1998)
head of government: Premier ZHU Rongji (since 18 March 1998); Vice Premiers QIAN Qichen (since 29 March 1993), LI Lanqing (29 March 1993), WU Bangguo (since 17 March 1995), and WEN Jiabao (since 18 March 1998)
cabinet: State Council appointed by the National People's Congress (NPC)
elections: president and vice president elected by the National People's Congress for five-year terms; elections last held 16–18 March 1998 (next to be held NA March 2003); premier nominated by the president, confirmed by the National People's Congress
election results: JIANG Zemin reelected president by the Ninth National People's Congress with a total of 2,882 votes (36 delegates voted against

him, 29 abstained, and 32 did not vote); HU Jintao elected vice president by the Ninth National People's Congress with a total of 2,841 votes (67 delegates voted against him, 39 abstained, and 32 did not vote)

Legislative branch: unicameral National People's Congress or Quanguo Renmin Daibiao Dahui (2,979 seats; members elected by municipal, regional, and provincial people's congresses to serve five-year terms)

elections: last held NA December 1997-NA February 1998 (next to be held late 2002-NA March 2003)

election results: percent of vote—NA%; seats—NA

Judicial branch: Supreme People's Court (judges appointed by the National People's Congress); Local Peoples Courts (comprise higher, intermediate and local courts); Special Peoples Courts (primarily military, maritime, and railway transport courts)

Political parties and leaders: Chinese Communist Party or CCP [JIANG Zemin, General Secretary of the Central Committee]; eight registered small parties controlled by CCP

Political pressure groups and leaders: no substantial political opposition groups exist, although the government has identified the Falun Gong sect and the China Democracy Party as potential rivals

International organization participation: AfDB, APEC, ARF (dialogue partner), AsDB, ASEAN (dialogue partner), BIS, CCC, CDB (non-regional), ESCAP, FAO, G-77, IAEA, IBRD, ICAO, ICC, ICFTU, ICRM, IDA, IFAD, IFC, IFRCS, IHO, ILO, IMF, IMO, Inmarsat, Intelsat, Interpol, IOC, ISO, ITU, LAIA (observer), MINURSO, NAM (observer), OPCW, PCA, UN, UN Security Council, UNAMSIL, UNCTAD, UNESCO, UNHCR, UNIDO, UNIKOM, UNITAR, UNMEE, UNTAET, UNTSO, UNU, UPU, WHO, WIPO, WMO, WToO, WTrO (observer), ZC

Diplomatic representation in the U.S.:

chief of mission: Ambassador-designate YANG Jiechi

chancery: 2300 Connecticut Avenue NW, Washington, DC 20008

telephone: [1] (202) 328-2500

consulate(s) general: Chicago, Houston, Los Angeles, New York, and San Francisco

Diplomatic representation from the U.S.:

chief of mission: Ambassador Clark T. RANDT, Jr.

embassy: Xiu Shui Bei Jie 3, 100600 Beijing

mailing address: PSC 461, Box 50, FPO AP 96521-0002

telephone: [86] (10) 6532-3431

FAX: [86] (10) 6532-6422

consulate(s) general: Chengdu, Guangzhou, Shanghai, Shenyang

Flag description: red with a large yellow five-pointed star and four smaller yellow five-pointed stars (arranged in a vertical arc toward the middle of the flag) in the upper hoist-side corner

Economy

Overview: In late 1978 the Chinese leadership began moving the economy from a sluggish Soviet-style centrally planned economy to a more market-oriented system. Whereas the system operates within a political framework of strict Communist control, the economic influence of non-state managers and enterprises has been steadily increasing. The authorities have switched to a system of household responsibility in agriculture in place of the old collectivization, increased the authority of local officials and plant managers in industry, permitted a wide variety of small-scale enterprise in services and light manufacturing, and opened the economy to increased foreign trade and investment. The result has been a quadrupling of GDP since 1978. In 2000, with its 1.26 billion people but a GDP of just $3,600 per capita, China stood as the second largest economy in the world after the U.S. (measured on a purchasing power parity basis). Agricultural output doubled in the 1980s, and industry also posted major gains, especially in coastal areas near Hong Kong and opposite Taiwan, where foreign investment helped spur output of both domestic and export goods. On the darker side, the leadership has often experienced in its hybrid system the worst results of socialism (bureaucracy and lassitude) and of capitalism (windfall gains and stepped-up inflation). Beijing thus has periodically backtracked, retightening central controls at intervals. The government has struggled to (a) collect revenues due from provinces, businesses, and individuals; (b) reduce corruption and other economic crimes; and (c) keep afloat the large state-owned enterprises many of which had been shielded from competition by subsides and had been losing the ability to pay full wages and pensions. From 80 to 120 million surplus rural workers are adrift between the villages and the cities, many subsisting through part-time low-paying jobs. Popular resistance, changes in central policy, and loss of authority by rural cadres have weakened China's population control program, which is essential to maintaining growth in living standards. Another long-term threat to continued rapid economic growth is the deterioration in the environment, notably air pollution, soil erosion, and the steady fall of the water table especially in the north. China continues to lose arable land because of erosion and economic development. Weakness in the global economy in 2001 could hamper growth in exports. Beijing will intensify efforts to stimulate growth through spending on infrastructure—such as water control and power grids—and poverty relief and through rural tax reform aimed at eliminating arbitrary local levies on farmers.

GDP: purchasing power parity—$4.5 trillion (2000 est.)

GDP—real growth rate: 8% (2000 est.)

GDP—per capita: purchasing power parity—$3,600 (2000 est.)

GDP—composition by sector:
agriculture: 15%
industry: 50%

services: 35% (2000 est.)

Population below poverty line: 10% (1999 est.)

Household income or consumption by percentage share:
lowest 10%: 2.4%
highest 10%: 30.4% (1998)

Inflation rate (consumer prices): 0.4% (2000 est.)

Labor force: 700 million (1998 est.)

Labor force—by occupation: agriculture 50%, industry 24%, services 26% (1998)

Unemployment rate: urban unemployment roughly 10%; substantial unemployment and underemployment in rural areas (2000 est.)

Budget:
revenues: $NA
expenditures: $NA, including capital expenditures of $NA

Industries: iron and steel, coal, machine building, armaments, textiles and apparel, petroleum, cement, chemical fertilizers, footwear, toys, food processing, automobiles, consumer electronics, telecommunications

Industrial production growth rate: 10% (2000 est.)

Electricity—production: 1.173 trillion kWh (1999)

Electricity—production by source:
fossil fuel: 79.82%
hydro: 18.98%
nuclear: 1.2%
other: 0.01% (1999)

Electricity—consumption: 1.084 trillion kWh (1999)

Electricity—exports: 7.2 billion kWh (1999)

Electricity—imports: 90 million kWh (1999)

Agriculture—products: rice, wheat, potatoes, sorghum, peanuts, tea, millet, barley, cotton, oilseed; pork; fish

Exports: $232 billion (f.o.b., 2000)

Exports—commodities: machinery and equipment; textiles and clothing, footwear, toys and sporting goods; mineral fuels

Exports—partners: U.S. 21%, Hong Kong 18%, Japan 17%, South Korea, Germany, Netherlands, UK, Singapore, Taiwan (2000)

Imports: $197 billion (f.o.b., 2000)

Imports—commodities: machinery and equipment, mineral fuels, plastics, iron and steel, chemicals

Imports—partners: Japan 18%, Taiwan 11%, U.S. 10%, South Korea 10%, Germany, Hong Kong, Russia, Malaysia (2000)

Debt—external: $162 billion (2000 est.)

Economic aid—recipient: $NA

Currency: yuan (CNY)

Currency code: CNY

Exchange rates: yuan per U.S. dollar—8.2776 (January 2001), 8.2785 (2000), 8.2783 (1999), 8.2790 (1998), 8.2898 (1997), 8.3142 (1996)

> *Note:* beginning 1 January 1994, the People's Bank of China quotes the midpoint rate against the U.S. dollar based on the previous day's prevailing rate in the interbank foreign exchange market

Fiscal year: calendar year

Communications

Telephones—main lines in use: 135 million (2000)

Telephones—mobile cellular: 65 million (January 2001)

Telephone system:

> *general assessment:* domestic and international services are increasingly available for private use; unevenly distributed domestic system serves principal cities, industrial centers, and many towns
> *domestic:* interprovincial fiber-optic trunk lines and cellular telephone systems have been installed; a domestic satellite system with 55 earth stations is in place
> *international:* satellite earth stations—5 Intelsat (4 Pacific Ocean and 1 Indian Ocean), 1 Intersputnik (Indian Ocean region) and 1 Inmarsat (Pacific and Indian Ocean regions); several international fiber-optic links to Japan, South Korea, Hong Kong, Russia, and Germany (2000)

Radio broadcast stations: AM 369, FM 259, shortwave 45 (1998)

Radios: 417 million (1997)

Television broadcast stations: 3,240 (of which 209 are operated by China Central Television, 31 are provincial TV stations and nearly 3,000 are local city stations) (1997)

Televisions: 400 million (1997)

Internet country code: .cn

Internet Service Providers (ISPs): 3 (2000)

Internet users: 22 million (January 2001)

Transportation

Railways:
   total: 67,524 km (including 5,400 km of provincial "local" rails)
   standard gauge: 63,924 km 1.435-m gauge (13,362 km electrified; 20,250 km double-track)
   narrow gauge: 3,600 km 0.750-m and 1.000-m gauge local industrial lines (1998 est.)
   note: a new total of 68,000 km was estimated for early 1999 to take new construction programs into account (1999)

Highways:
   total: 1.4 million km
   paved: 271,300 km (with at least 16,000 km of expressways)
   unpaved: 1,128,700 km (1999)

Waterways: 110,000 km (1999)

Pipelines: crude oil 9,070 km; petroleum products 560 km; natural gas 9,383 km (1998)

Ports and harbors: Dalian, Fuzhou, Guangzhou, Haikou, Huangpu, Lianyungang, Nanjing, Nantong, Ningbo, Qingdao, Qinhuangdao, Shanghai, Shantou, Tianjin, Xiamen, Xingang, Yantai, Zhanjiang

Merchant marine:
   total: 1,745 ships (1,000 GRT or over) totaling 16,533,521 GRT/24,746,859 DWT
   ships by type: barge carrier 2, bulk 324, cargo 825, chemical tanker 21, combination bulk 11, combination ore/oil 1, container 132, liquefied gas 24, multi-functional large-load carrier 5, passenger 7, passenger/cargo 45, petroleum tanker 258, refrigerated cargo 22, roll on/roll off 23, short-sea passenger 41, specialized tanker 3, vehicle carrier 1 (2000 est.)

Airports: 489 (2000 est.)

Airports—with paved runways:
   total: 324
   over 3,047 m: 27
   2,438 to 3,047 m: 88
   1,524 to 2,437 m: 147
   914 to 1,523 m: 30
   under 914 m: 32 (2000 est.)

Airports—with unpaved runways:
   total: 165
   over 3,047 m: 1
   2,438 to 3,047 m: 1
   1,524 to 2,437 m: 29
   914 to 1,523 m: 56

under 914 m: 78 (2000 est.)

Military

Military branches: People's Liberation Army (PLA)—which includes Ground Forces, Navy (includes Marines and Naval Aviation), Air Force, Second Artillery Corps (the strategic missile force), People's Armed Police (internal security troops, nominally subordinate to Ministry of Public Security, but included by the Chinese as part of the "armed forces" and considered to be an adjunct to the PLA in wartime)

Military manpower—military age: 18 years of age

Military manpower—availability: males age 15–49: 366,306,353 (2001 est.)

Military manpower—fit for military service: males age 15–49: 200,886,946 (2001 est.)

Military manpower—reaching military age annually: males: 10,089,458 (2001 est.)

Military expenditures—dollar figure: $12.608 billion (FY99); *note—* China's real defense spending may be several times higher than the official figure because a number of significant items are funded elsewhere

Military expenditures—percent of GDP: 1.2% (FY99)

Transnational Issues

Disputes—international: most of boundary with India in dispute; dispute over at least two small sections of the boundary with Russia remains to be settled, despite 1997 boundary agreement; portions of the boundary with Tajikistan are indefinite; 33-km section of boundary with North Korea in the Paektu-san (mountain) area is indefinite; involved in a complex dispute over the Spratly Islands with Malaysia, Philippines, Taiwan, Vietnam, and possibly Brunei; maritime boundary agreement with Vietnam in the Gulf of Tonkin awaits ratification; Paracel Islands occupied by China, but claimed by Vietnam and Taiwan; claims Japanese-administered Senkaku-shoto (Senkaku Islands/Diaoyu Tai), as does Taiwan

Illicit drugs: major transshipment point for heroin produced in the Golden Triangle; growing domestic drug abuse problem; source country for chemical precursors and methamphetamine

Bibliography

Books

Baum, Richard. *Burying Mao: Chinese Politics in the Age of Deng Xiaoping*. Princeton, NJ: Princeton University Press, 1994.

Becker, Jasper. *The Chinese*. New York: Free Press, 2000.

Chang, Maria Hsia. *Return of the Dragon: China's Wounded Nationalism*. Boulder, CO: Westview Press, 2001.

Cohen, Warren I. *America's Response to China: A History of Sino-American Relations*. New York: Columbia University Press, 2000.

Courtois, Stéphane, et al. *The Black Book of Communism: Crimes, Terror, Repression*. Cambridge, MA: Harvard University Press, 1999.

Evans, Richard. *Deng Xiaoping and the Making of Modern China*. New York: Viking, 1994.

Garver, John W. *Protracted Contest: Sino-Indian Rivalry in the Twentieth Century*. Seattle: University of Washington Press, 2001.

Gertz, Bill. *The China Threat: How the People's Republic Targets America*. Washington, D.C.: Regnery Publishing, 2000.

Gilley, Bruce. *Tiger on the Brink: Jiang Zemin and China's New Elite*. Berkeley: University of California Press, 1998.

Glassman, Ronald M. *China in Transition: Communism, Capitalism, and Democracy*. New York: Praeger, 1991.

Goldman, Merle. *Sowing the Seeds of Democracy in China: Political Reform in the Deng Xiaoping Era*. Cambridge, MA: Harvard University Press, 1994.

Hsing, You-tien. *Making Capitalism in China: The Taiwan Connection*. New York: Oxford University Press, 1998.

Lam, Willy Wo-Lap. *The Era of Jiang Zemin*. New York: Prentice Hall, 1999.

Lardy, Nicholas R. *Integrating China into the Global Economy*. Washington, D.C.: Brookings Institution Press, 2002.

Murray, Geoffrey. *China: The Next Superpower*. New York: St. Martin's Press, 1998.

Norbu, Dawa. *China's Tibet Policy*. Richmond, Surrey: Curzon Press, 2001.

Ogden, Suzanne. *Inklings of Democracy in China*. Cambridge, MA: Harvard University Asia Center, 2002.

Peterson, Glen, Ruth Hayhoe, and Yongling Lu, eds. *Education, Culture, and Identity in Twentieth-century China*. Ann Arbor: University of Michigan Press, 2001.

Sheng, Lijun. *China's Dilemma: The Taiwan Issue*. Singapore: Institute of Southeast Asian Studies, 2001.

Short, Philip. *Mao: A Life*. New York: Henry Holt, 2000.

Sinkule, Barbara, and Leonard Ortolano. *Implementing Environmental Policy in China*. Westport, CT: Praeger, 1995.

Starr, John Bryan. *Understanding China: A Guide to China's Economy, History, and Political Structure*. New York: Hill and Wang, 2001.

Studwell, Joe. *The China Dream: The Quest for the Last Great Untapped Market on Earth*. New York: Atlantic Monthly Press, 2002.

Subramanian, R. R. *India, Pakistan, China: Defence and Nuclear Tangle in South Asia*. New Delhi: ABC Publishing House, 1989.

Tyler, Patrick E. *A Great Wall: Six Presidents and China*. New York: Public Affairs, 1999.

Wang, Mei-ling T. *The Dust That Never Settles: The Taiwan Independence Campaign and U.S.-China Relations*. Lanham, MD: University Press of America, 1999.

Wishnick, Elizabeth. *Mending Fences: The Evolution of Moscow's China Policy, from Brezhnev to Yeltsin*. Seattle: University of Washington Press, 2001

Wu, Hongda Harry, and George Vecsey. *Troublemaker: One Man's Crusade against China's Cruelty*. New York: Times Books, 1996.

Zhao, Suisheng, ed. *China and Democracy: The Prospects for a Democratic China*. New York: Routledge, 2000.

Web Sites

Readers who would like additional information about China should consult the following Web sites, which are operational as of this writing.

Beijing Review

www.bjreview.com.cn
This is the Web site of the English-language *Beijing Review* magazine, which is published weekly in China and contains many informative articles about current Chinese domestic and foreign policy issues. Articles from past issues are also archived on the site.

Chinasite.com

www.chinasite.com
This Internet portal provides links to nearly 3,500 Web sites devoted to China.

China Institute

www.chinainstitute.org
This is the official site of the China Institute, a nonprofit organization in New York City. Established in 1926, the China Institute promotes the enjoyment and understanding of contemporary Chinese culture and civilization through seminars, art exhibits, and classroom projects. The site details the China Institute's activities and services.

China News Agency

www.chinanewsagency.com
An affiliate of the World News Network, the China News Agency covers China and links to different news sites in the West and China.

China-on-Site

www.china-on-site.com
This site provides information about Chinese literature, music, painting, gardening, and cooking.

China Pages

www.chinapages.com
This site provides economic news about China.

China Today

www.chinatoday.com
China Today is a comprehensive on-line resource that provides information about a wide range of topics, such as China's history, culture, geography, government, legal system, and military.

China Vista

www.chinavista.com

This site provides cultural and travel information about China.

Embassy of the People's Republic of China in the United States of America

http://www.china-embassy.org/eng/index.html

This is the official site of China's diplomatic mission to the United States in Washington, D.C. The site provides basic facts about China, information about visiting China, and the Chinese government's views on several important issues, such as U.S.-Chinese relations, Taiwan, Tibet, the Falun Gong, and human rights.

Government of Tibet in Exile

www.tibet.com

This is the official Web site of Tibet's government in exile, which is headed by the Dalai Lama. The site offers information about Tibet's history and culture and China's occupation of the country since 1950, including the persecution of the Tibetan people.

Human Rights in China

www.hric.org

With offices in New York City and Hong Kong, this organization promotes the respect of human rights in China and reports acts of persecution by the Chinese government against political dissidents and religious groups on its site.

Xinhua News Agency

http://www.xinhuanet.com/english/

Xinhua is China's official news agency, providing daily coverage of domestic and international news in many different languages from the government's perspective.

Additional Periodical Articles with Abstracts

More information about China can be found in the following articles. Readers who are interested in additional articles may consult *The Readers' Guide to Periodical Literature* and other H.W. Wilson publications.

The Great Upward. James Pinkerton. *American Spectator*, v. 35 pp38–9 March–April 2002.

Pinkerston writes that Americans should take heed of the latest news about the Chinese space program. China appears to be engaging a long-term perspective on developments in space, and America's failure to deal in long-time frames may ultimately mean losing to those who do consider the distant future. If the Chinese are serious in their references to space as a fourth frontier, then their failure to look outward and fill a geopolitical vacuum in the last millennium could be rectified in the astro-political vacuum. By contrast, America is a young country and has yet to prove that it can sustain a long march through history. The question now is whether the United States can learn from a country that is older and perhaps wiser.

NASA Eyes China Ties As New Shenzhou Flies. Craig Covault. *Aviation Week and Space Technology*, v. 156 pp27–8 April 1, 2002.

Covault writes that the Bush administration is embarking on a reassessment of U.S.-Chinese space cooperation. NASA administrator Sean O'Keefe told a forum in Washington, D.C., that he and the deputy secretary of state, Richard Armitage, are spending considerable time exploring whether and how to bring China into closer cooperation with the United States on space projects. The announcement came two days after the March 25, 2002, launch of the third unmanned flight test of China's Shenzhou manned vehicle, which will carry the first Chinese astronauts into space over the next one to two years. The United States has never had any space cooperation with China, and to have the opening of U.S. space cooperation with China addressed at the deputy secretary of state level is extremely significant.

No Breakthrough on Chinese Proliferation. Paul Mann. *Aviation Week and Space Technology,* v. 156 pp57–9 March 11, 2002.

According to the writer, the United States and China are still at loggerheads over Beijing's export of ballistic missile expertise to unstable nations and pariah dictatorships. President George W. Bush and Chinese president Jiang Zemin reiterated at their Beijing summit on February 21–22, 2002, what the White House calls their "vital" cooperation on intelligence and law enforcement in the wake of September 11. The Bush administration's hopes of ending Chinese missile proliferation and achieving something more stable were dashed at the latest Bush-Jiang meeting. White House officials claim the main problem is the lack of an export control law in China. The United States alleges that Chinese companies regularly violate the multinational Missile Technology Control Regime, which China has not signed, but has pledged to adhere to the "contours" of the agreement.

China's Carmakers: Flattened by Falling Tariffs. Dexter Roberts. *Business Week,* p51 December 3, 2001.

Roberts asserts that China's membership in the World Trade Organization (WTO) means stiffer competition from imports for domestic carmakers. The WTO will force China to greatly reduce tariffs on imported cars. In 2002 alone, sedan imports are expected to increase 50 percent, to 120,000. Jia Xinguang, a researcher at the China National Automotive Industry Consulting and Development Corp., predicts that, as a result of this, car prices should fall by one-third in a few years.

Sea Change on China. Pete Engardio, Stan Crock, and Mark L. Clifford. *Business Week,* pp59–9 May 21, 2001.

The writers report that several conservatives in President Bush's administration are taking a hard line against China. The officials believe that Washington has been far too complacent with regard to China's intent to take Taiwan by force, a conflict that would surely involve America. Although Washington remains in favor of a strong commercial relationship and collaboration with China on issues where the two nations' interests overlap, the U.S. is attempting to encourage other Asian powers to join its missile defense plan. It remains to be seen whether America's new policy will backfire. So far, Beijing has responded mainly with propaganda, but China watchers are predicting that, before long, it will begin striking back. Its options range from recommencing the sale of arms to American rivals such as Iraq to overwhelming any U.S. missile shield by extending its own nuclear program.

China: Coping with Its New Power. Mark Clifford, Dexter Roberts, and Pete Engardio. *Business Week,* pp28–34 April 16, 2001.

The writers assert that the United States faces a complex foreign policy quandary with China, Asia's rising superpower. In March 2001, negotiations dramatically narrowed the differences between the two countries over the agricultural and insurance issues that had been delaying China's long quest to enter the World Trade Organization (WTO). If all progressed smoothly, China had high hopes that the final details would be hammered out in late April in meetings with the United States and other trade partners. The April 1, 2001, collision of a U.S. EP-3E spy plane with a Chinese fighter has, however, snowballed into another crisis. Whether or not this matter is resolved, the nasty slide in U.S.-Chinese relations could continue. Leaders on both sides have every reason to prevent events from spinning out of control, but both President Bush and President Jiang Zemin are being pushed by hard-liners in their own governments and by public opinion to stand firm.

"New" China: Same Old Tricks. Tony Carnes. *Christianity Today,* v. 46 pp38–42 March 11, 2002.

Carnes writes about the persecution of Christians in China. Activist Li Shi-xiong, a Chinese Christian refugee and head of the New York City–based Committee for Investigation on Persecution of Religion in China, has compiled an extensive new archive documenting brutal religious persecution. He believes that the documents establish that Communist rulers at the highest levels take an active role in persecuting house-church Christians. Top leaders in the country have blamed repression on overzealous local officials in the past. The archive contains 22,000 testimonies about persecution of Chinese Christians and includes court transcripts, internal government documents, and photographs. Experts say that it is the largest collection ever assembled on the persecuted church in China, and Li and the New York committee believe that going public with it will build international political pressure on China's leaders to end their repression of religion.

Class Participation. Peter Phillips Simpson. *Commonweal,* v. 129 pp11–12 April 5, 2002.

The writer, who has taught political philosophy at Beijing's Renmin University of China, discusses his belief that his controversial remarks about Communism, Chairman Mao, and the Vietnam War have provoked his students into thought.

China's Media: Betweem Politics and the Market. Judy   Polumbaum. *Current History,* v. 100 pp269–77 September 2001.

Polumbaum writes that the impression that freedom of expression in China is severely restricted is persistent, but if the health of a society can be gauged by the quantity and variety of information available, then the country is in far better shape than the images of a propaganda state suggest. Certainly, some spheres of investigation are still treacherous, certain issues and individuals are beyond question or reproach, and certain subjects are presented in a rigidly conformist and often strident way. The officially sanctioned stories are, however, but the most obvious outcroppings of an extensive media landscape featuring many other formations, including celebrity gossip, home remodeling advice, and sports news. The boundaries on the production and dissemination of news, entertainment, and information have been steadily eroding for two decades.

Cracks in the Wall: China's Eroding Coercive State. Murray   Scot   Tanner. *Current History,* v. 100 pp243–9 September 2001.

Tanner asserts that beneath the surface, China's state coercive system is facing unprecedented challenges that could create a crisis of governability for Beijing in the next decade. The challenges to the apparatus, which includes the Public Security and State Security organs, come from, among other things, increasing demonstrations and strikes. The uneven erosion and dissipation of the state's coercive and law enforcement systems poses serious and complex implications for both the Chinese Communist Party's ability to survive and China's prospects of undergoing a stable transition to a democratic system anytime soon. It also creates serious foreign policy implications for America and other countries that must deal with China on numerous enforcement issues.

The Challenge from China. Kerry A. Dolan and Quentin Hardy. *Forbes,* v. 169 pp72–6 May 13, 2002.

The authors discuss the intention of Chinese companies to build their brands for the American market of the future. Chinese companies got their first taste of the

U.S. market two decades ago, when it seemed as if half the products in Wal-Mart were made in China for U.S. brands. A handful of powerful Chinese exporters are looking to sell goods under their own brand names and target the extra profits that a distinctive name brings. U.S. companies hailed China's entry into the WTO, eyeing lower tariffs and a huge waiting market, but WTO membership also means fewer restrictions on China's apparel exports worldwide. Smart Chinese companies facing harsher competition in their home market intend to keep growing by taking their products abroad. Five or ten years in the future, Chinese firms that have found their place, leveraged their formidable manufacturing prowess, and mastered Western-style marketing could become household names in the United States.

The U.S. and China: Seven Pillars of Wisdom. Paul Johnson. *Forbes,* v. 167 p49 June 11, 2001.

Johnson writes that it is clear that getting on sensibly with China will be one of the biggest challenges of George W. Bush's presidency. Seven pillars of wisdom that should be the axioms of U.S.-China policy are: U.S. policy should strengthen China economically and weaken it militarily; China must be brought to believe that its manifest destiny lies in Asia; the United States should stress the importance of the rule of law; the United States should do everything in its power to draw China into the international law-making process; the United States must be careful to carry the support and cooperation of other powerful and influential Asian powers; China is never as strong as it looks and never as weak as it looks; and China wants to emerge once more on the world stage as the living custodian and repository of one of the world's great civilizations. Washington policymakers must discover what the genuine Chinese public opinion is.

Facing Reality in China Policy. David Shambaugh. *Foreign Affairs,* v. 80 pp50–64 January–February 2001.

Shambaugh asserts that the most significant country in America's future may be China. Given China's indubitable increase in power, Washington must accord it due attention. Although U.S.-China relations have recently advanced considerably, especially on trade-related issues, existing tensions could spark conflict at any time. President Bush's foreign policy and security team should concentrate on both the current U.S.-China agenda and the wider issue of the U.S.-China relationship, but first the administration must tackle some urgent problems. Shambaugh outlines the immediate issues faced by the new administration, including the Taiwan situation, America's pursuit of a national missile defense, the evolving situation on the Korean Peninsula, China's proliferation of nuclear technology and missile components, human rights and the rule of law in China, and China's membership in the WTO.

The Tiananmen Papers. Andrew J. Nathan. *Foreign Affairs,* v. 80 pp2–48 January–February 2001.

The author discusses the secret documents revealing the inner workings of China's Communist Party leadership during the 1989 Tiananmen Square crisis that have recently surfaced. The documents were smuggled out of China by a supporter of Communist Party members who believe that challenging the official image of Tiananmen as a legitimate suppression of a violent antigovernment riot will spark a resumption of political reform. The materials vividly describe the conflict between hard-liners and reformers on how to tackle the student protests that swept China that year. In an article adapted from the forthcoming book *The Tiananmen Papers: The Chinese Leadership's Decision to Use Force against Their Own People—In Their Own Words*, Nathan and his co-author Liang Zhang examine the reaction to the student protests of President Yang Shangkun and leading officials Deng Xiaoping, Zhao Ziyang, Jiang Zemin, and Li Peng.

Sweet and Sour Deal. Nicolas R. Lardy. *Foreign Policy,* pp20–21 March–April 2002.

According to Lardy, trade officials from the United States, Europe, and Japan have portrayed China's entry into the WTO in December 2001 as an antidote to their increasing trade deficits with China, but the reality is that China's agreement to drop tariffs, phase out import quotas, open new sectors of its economy to foreign investment, and otherwise follow WTO rules will not reverse this imbalance in trade. China's trade boom is due in part to the growing importance of the U.S. export market, which caused the U.S. bilateral deficit with China to reach an estimated $84.4 billion in 2001. This deficit is likely to keep growing for now because the effects of China's market opening are likely to be swamped by the displacement effect, as China becomes the preferred location for making the labor-intensive goods of more and more global firms. In the short term, China's integration into the global economy will probably take its heaviest toll on other Asian countries.

It's All Made in China Now. Bill Powell. *Fortune,* v. 145 pp121–8 March 4, 2002.

According to Powell, China's rapid growth up the technology ladder has massive consequences for the global economy. A steady stream of foreign direct investment, apparently unaffected by global macroeconomic cycles, is recasting the country's industrial base. It is safe to say that the world, especially Japan and the rest of Asia, will never be the same. Ten years ago, China's endless supply of inexpensive labor produced an endless supply of cheap, and often shoddy, products, such as toys and textiles. It still makes such products, but it also does a lot more besides. In Shanghai's Pudong industrial zone, there are new factories for as far as the eye can see. Investors include Intel, Corning, and OMRON. China's emergence as a reliable, stable producer of high-value, technologically sophisticated products will alter the economics of a wide range of manufacturing industries. In fact, that process is already well established.

Habeas Corpus. Guoqi Wang. *Harper's,* v. 304 pp22–5 February 2002.

An excerpt is reprinted from testimony delivered last summer by Guoqi Wang, a former doctor at a Chinese People's Liberation Army hospital, to the subcommittee on international operations and human rights of the U.S. House of Representatives. China has executed over 5,000 people in the past year, more than all other nations together, frequently for crimes like tax evasion. Organs are regularly harvested from executed prisoners, and earnings from transplants are believed to earn Chinese hospitals tens of millions of dollars per year. The writer, who removed skin and corneas from the corpses of more than 100 executed prisoners and, in a couple of cases, victims of intentionally botched executions, describes the procedure for organ recovery.

Bush's China Opening. Peter Kwong and Dusanka Miscevic. *The Nation,* v. 274 p26 March 4, 2002.

According to the writer, there are long-term problems hidden behind China's new friendly attitude toward America. Since September 11, China has changed from being the most outspoken adversary of the United States to being its highly appreciated ally. China's rapid economic expansion and increasing political influence in Asia have placed it on a collision course with the United States, however, causing nationalistic posturing and encouraging military spending in both nations. Economically, Chinese imports are creating a major trade deficit for the United States—its biggest with any trading partner, including Japan. If China is to become a stable and reliable long-term ally in the region, Americans will have to stop their cowboy swaggering, which has recently aroused strong anti-American sentiment among the Chinese, and use the lull in mutual antagonism to ensure that American corporate interests do not ignore labor and human rights abuses.

China: A Reality Check. John Derbyshire. *National Review,* v. 53 pp38–43 September 17, 2001.

Derbyshire asserts that China's present dictatorship is firmly established. Although the level of discontent in China is high, it does not threaten the leadership. China's urban middle classes—supposedly the driving force of political reform—are ambivalent about Communism. Even at its most mendacious, Communist Party propaganda has been highly successful, and huge numbers of Chinese people believe what the party tells them to believe. Furthermore, the apparatus of terror is still intact, and the "fear factor" remains an important element in Chinese life. The Communists may well ride out present dangers and maintain enough public support, or at least indifference, to see them safely through WTO accession and into the future to a triumphant and well-organized Olympic extravaganza that will solidify their hold on China.

The Internet in China: A New Fantasy. Jisi Wang. *New Perspectives Quarterly,* v. 18 pp22–4 Winter 2001.

According to the writer, in China, the Internet is far from being a practical and effective instrument for those who want to stage a political act or promote a political idea. The speedy growth of IT industries was strongly supported by governmental policies and funds, and by July 2000, 16.9 million Chinese had access to the Web. Online Chinese account for only 1.3 percent of the total population, however, and a typical Web surfer might be a single male who has recently obtained a bachelor's degree, taken a job in an IT business, and who will gladly spend 5 percent to 10 percent of his income on Internet access. Moreover, most of these people are hardly experienced or even interested in politics. In the early stages of a civil society's development, the opening of new channels of communication clears the way to well-intended and conducive exchange of ideas. Unfortunately, the Internet's anonymity allows for vulgar curses and humiliating attacks on a large range of individuals and organizations.

A New Europe Has Its Own Agenda with China. Chris Patten. *New Perspectives Quarterly,* v. 18 pp24–6 Summer 2001.

Patten writes that Europe and China must reexamine their shared concerns in the face of rapid change. New areas such as illegal immigration, food hygiene, and genetically modified organisms join an agenda already dominated by energy policy, China being the world's second-largest consumer of energy and its third-largest producer. Other issues, such as the information society, complement the traditional development and trade themes that have dictated the European approach since relations were established in 1975. The European Union's success in implementing an effective multilateral system depends on close cooperation with the major players and encouragement of the international engagement of bodies such as the United Nations.

China: The Anaconda in the Chandelier. Perry Link. *New York Review of Books,* v. 49 pp67–70 April 11, 2002.

Link writes that although informal speech in China is much freer than in the past, repression remains an important problem. The highest priority of the top leadership of China's Communist Party is to retain power, which leads it to ban any public expression of opposition to itself and to crush groups that it does not control or could not easily control if it had to. Censorship in China involves a fear, a dull, well-entrenched leeriness of taking the risk to express a politically sensitive idea in public, for example. The controlling power of this fear is impressive, compelling people to censor themselves and scholars to lie low, overseas businessmen working in China to pull punches, and lawyers to mince words. As China's international involvement continues to grow, however, it becomes vital for the rest of the world to notice this problem and discern its effects on the flood of reliable information between China and other countries.

China Emerges As Rival to U.S. in Asian Trade. Jane Perlez. *New York Times,* ppA1+ June 28, 2002.

The writer discusses China's attempts to replace the U.S. as the leading trading partner in Asia.

Order Yields to Lawlessness As Maoism Recedes in China. Erik Eckholm. *New York Times,* ppA1+ May 29, 2002.

Eckholm reports that widespread lawlessness has grown in many of China's towns and villages in the last two decades as the once stringent Maoist discipline has withered and often been replaced by an economic free-for-all that is devoid of public cohesion or shared ideals. Senior Beijing leaders and the official news media have begun to acknowledge the problem, repeatedly condemning cowed and corrupt police departments that function as protective umbrellas for criminals.

In Rural China, Mental Hospitals Await Some Who Rock the Boat.

Elisabeth Rosenthal. *New York Times,* ppA1+ February 16, 2002.

Rosenthal writes that although China's two-and-a-half year crackdown on the Falun Gong movement has generated concern over the misuse of psychiatry, little evidence exists to suggest that it is routinely used on political dissidents. However, it is quite commonly used by local governments to silence the shrill voices of those who aggressively press the government with their protests and petitions. The ordeal of Huang Shurong, a resident of Heilongjiang Province, is discussed.

China.org. Joe Klein. *New Yorker,* v. 77 p53–4 April 23, 2001.

Klein reports that on March 15, 2001, Chinese Prime Minister Zhu Rongji made a public apology in Beijing after a mysterious explosion in a Jiangxi Province school left 42 people, including 38 children, dead. The students, aged between nine and eleven, had probably been making fireworks in a forced "work-study" program designed to help pay the local school budget. There is no tradition of public apology by Chinese leaders, and while Zhu apologized for the explosion, he did not reject the official government story that the blast had been caused by a mad bomber. The apology was particularly important, however, because Zhu had been forced by the power of public opinion to efface himself.

The Conflict to Come. Evan Thomas and John Barry. *Newsweek,* v. 137 pp20–4 April 23, 2001.

The writers argue that the United States could soon face a new era of confrontation with China. The 24-member crew of the U.S. EP-3E spy plane held by the Chinese for 11 days after they were forced to make an emergency landing at the Chinese air base on Hainan Island returned home recently to a heroes' welcome. The plane was forced to land on Hainan after a midair collision with a Chinese military plane, in which the Chinese pilot died. After narrowly escaping a hostage crisis, President Bush realizes that he must pay careful attention to a fraught relationship with an increasingly difficult adversary. Pentagon security planners see the collision as proof of a long-brewing belief that China hopes to achieve dominance of the seas around its territory and push the United States out. Beijing's harassment of American spy planes could alert the Bush administration to the weakness of the United States' strategic position in Asia, which could increase the probability of a future confrontation between the two countries.

China Wakes up a Tiger. Mahlon Meyer. *Newsweek,* v. 137 pp32–3 February 5, 2001.

Meyer warns that China's repression of Falun Gong could turn a spiritual movement into a political opposition. Falun Gong is a movement dedicated to a diverse mix of mysticism, meditation, and slow-motion exercise. It has no political agenda, and its sole charismatic figure—Li Hongzhi, the 49-year-old founder—lives quietly in exile in America. Despite this, there has been an ongoing brutal crackdown on people who, in most other countries, would be considered harmless idealists. This is because, with the Chinese Communist Party ideology in tatters, the government feels threatened by any organization that can attract millions of people to a set of ideals. By repressing Falun Gong, however, the party risks labeling millions of Chinese as enemies of the regime and politicizing a movement that originally had nothing to do with politics.

China's America Problem. Ying Ma. *Policy Review,* pp43–56 February–March 2002.

The author writes that gloating from the Chinese people in the aftermath of the September 11 terrorist attacks on the United States is profoundly disturbing. In chat rooms, many Chinese Web users declared the attacks to be a payback for America's imperialistic foreign policy and rejoiced at the sight of the "world's policeman" being dealt an enormous blow. This attitude is very disquieting given that these are the people on whose behalf U.S. policymakers have sought freedom and democracy in the past 12 years. Moreover, the fact that the gloating comes from the Chinese Internet generation is even more unsettling because this small but fast-growing population has been widely hailed by the Chinese and U.S. governments as the bright future of a more modern, open, and free 21st-century China. At this time of constant national soul-searching over the nature and worth of U.S. foreign policy, a close examination of the severe disconnect between Washington and the Chinese people is essential.

China Debates Big Drop in Women Physics Majors. Yang Jianxiang. *Science,* v. 295 p263 January 11, 2002.

The writer reports that a great decline in the number of women physics majors is prompting debate among Chinese academics. During the 1970s, women accounted for more than one-third of the physics majors at top Chinese universities; that proportion has since plummeted to less than one in 10, a figure even lower than that in the West. However, whereas some academics are concerned at this precipitous decline, others are arguing that, in reality, the earlier numbers were greatly inflated, as students were not free to choose the subjects they would study but were compelled to enter fields dictated by the government, according to what it felt was needed by the country at the time. Others argue that the sharp decline is due to negative messages conveyed in the media and reinforced by the education and employment systems.

China's Lifestyle Choice. Hannah Beech. *Time,* v. 158 p32 August 6, 2001.

Beech writes that China may have solved its population problem, but it was been replaced by a host of new ones. The average Chinese woman now has two children, compared with six children 30 years ago. According to United Nations projections, the population of China will begin to decline in 2042. In Chinese cities, the one-child policy has developed into a no-child philosophy. This news has spurred China's normally apathetic parliament, which has proposed changing the one-child policy to enable some urban couples to have a second child. It would be left to each province to determine the birth control procedures that best matched its circumstances. The change is desperately needed because the coddled offspring of the one-child policy are reaching adulthood, and many show little sense of family obligation. China's aging population is predicted to peak in 2040, and there is no established mechanism to finance its welfare.

The China Question. Joshua Kurlantzick. *U. S. News & World Report,* v. 132 pp42–6 February 11, 2002.

Kurlantzick writes that China's wealth gap will help determine the fate of globalization. If it can adapt to international trading rules and move into higher-value industries, while reducing internal equality and quelling social unrest, China may become a robust engine of world growth. The income gap may be a ticking time bomb, however. Today, about 160 million rural Chinese are unemployed. Moreover, after joining the WTO last year, China promised to slash tariffs, changes that could decimate farmers and increase unemployment in the country's center. Last year, rural protests across the country led to more than 4,000 injuries and deaths from battles between rural residents and security forces. If left unchecked, that tension could derail China's global momentum. Despite the scary scenarios, most foreign business people believe China will mature into a responsible trading partner.

On the Trail of a Killer. Bay Fang. *U. S. News & World Report,* v. 131 pp22–6 September 6, 2001.

The author reports that China is facing a spreading HIV-AIDS epidemic. Until now, Beijing has been in a willful state of denial, with China officially reporting just 26,058 people infected with HIV. In response to foreign criticism, authorities recently acknowledged that the real number may exceed 600,000. Foreign experts warn that if more is not done to slow the spread of HIV, more than 10 million will be infected by 2010. The Chinese government has concentrated on fighting drug trafficking but has done little else because it does not want to admit how far the AIDS crisis has spread.

Index